THE ULTIM TEFAL DUAL AIR FRYER COOKBOOK

1900 Days of Easy and Delicious Air Fryer Recipes for Beginners | Cook Faster and Healthier with Your Tefal EasyFry 2-Drawers

Ann R. Gaither

CONTENTS

MEASUREMENT CONVERSIONS

BASIC KITCHEN CONVERSIONS & EQUIVALENTS

DRY MEASUREMENTS CONVERSION CHART

3 TEASPOONS = 1 TABLESPOON = 1/16 CUP
6 TEASPOONS = 2 TABLESPOONS = 1/8 CUP
12 TEASPOONS = 4 TABLESPOONS = 1/4 CUP
24 TEASPOONS = 8 TABLESPOONS = 1/2 CUP
36 TEASPOONS = 12 TABLESPOONS = 3/4 CUP
48 TEASPOONS = 16 TABLESPOONS = 1 CUP

METRIC TO US COOKING CONVER-SIONS

OVEN TEMPERATURES

120 °C = 250 °F
160 °C = 320 °F
180 °C = 350 °F
205 °C = 400 °F
220 °C = 425 °F

LIQUID MEASUREMENTS CONVERSION CHART

8 FLUID OUNCES = 1 CUP = 1/2 PINT = 1/4 QUART
16 FLUID OUNCES = 2 CUPS = 1 PINT = 1/2 QUART
32 FLUID OUNCES = 4 CUPS = 2 PINTS = 1 QUART
1/4 GALLON
128 FLUID OUNCES = 16 CUPS = 8 PINTS = 4 QUARTS = 1 GALLON

BAKING IN GRAMS

1 CUP FLOUR = 140 GRAMS
1 CUP SUGAR = 150 GRAMS
1 CUP POWDERED SUGAR=160 GRAMS
1 CUP HEAVY CREAM = 235 GRAMS

VOLUME

1 MILLILITER=1/5 TEASPOON
5 ML = 1 TEASPOON
15 ML = 1 TABLESPOON
240 ML = 1 CUP OR 8 FLUID OUNCES
1 LITER=34 FL. OUNCES

WEIGHT

1 GRAM = 035 OUNCES
100 GRAMS=3.5 OUNCES
500 GRAMS = 1.1 POUNDS
1 KILOGRAM=35 OUNCES

US TO METRIC COOKING CONVERSIONS

1/5 TSP = 1 ML
1 TSP=5 ML
1 TBSP = 15 ML
1 FL OUNCE = 30 ML
1 CUP=237 ML
1 PINT (2 CUPS) = 473 ML
1 QUART (4 CUPS)=.95 LITER
1GALLON (16 CUPS)=3.8LITERS
1 0Z=28 GRAMS
1 POUND = 454 GRAMS

BUTTER

1 CUP BUTTER=2 STICKS = 8 OUNCES = 230 GRAMS=8 TABLESPOONS

WHAT DOES 1 CUP EQUAL

1 CUP = 8 FLUID OUNCES
1 CUP = 16 TABLESPOONS
1 CUP = 48 TEASPOONS
1 CUP = 1/2 PINT
1 CUP = 1/4 QUART
1 CUP = 1/16 GALLON
1 CUP = 240 ML

BAKING PAN CONVERSIONS

1 CUP ALL-PURPOSE FLOUR=4.5 OZ
1 CUP ROLLED OATS = 3 OZ 1 LARGE EGG = 1.7 OZ
1 CUP BUTTER=80Z 1 CUP MILK = 8 OZ
1 CUP HEAVY CREAM = 8.4 OZ
1 CUP GRANULATED SUGAR=7.1 OZ
1 CUP PACKED BROWN SUGAR = 7.75 OZ
1 CUP VEGETABLE OIL = 7.7 OZ
1 CUP UNSIFTED POWDERED SUGAR = 4.4 OZ

BAKING PAN CONVERSIONS

9-INCH ROUND CAKE PAN= 12 CUPS
10-INCH TUBE PAN =16 CUPS
11-INCH BUNDT PAN = 12 CUPS
9-INCH SPRINGFORM PAN = 10 CUPS
9 X 5 INCH LOAF PAN=8 CUPS
9-INCH SQUARE PAN=8 CUPS

Snacks And Appetizers Recipes

Crab Cake Poppers

Servings: 6
Cooking Time: 15 Minutes
Ingredients:

- 1 egg, lightly beaten
- 453g lump crab meat, drained
- 1 tsp garlic, minced
- 1 tsp lemon juice
- 1 tsp old bay seasoning
- 30g almond flour
- 1 tsp Dijon mustard
- 28g mayonnaise
- Pepper
- Salt

Directions:

1. In a bowl, mix crab meat and remaining ingredients until well combined.
2. Make small balls from the crab meat mixture and place them on a plate.
3. Place the plate in the refrigerator for 50 minutes.
4. Insert a crisper plate in the Tefal air fryer baskets.
5. Place the prepared crab meatballs in both baskets.
6. Select zone 1 then select "air fry" mode and set the temperature to 360 degrees F for 10 minutes. Press "match" to match zone 2 settings to zone 1. Press "start/stop" to begin.

Crispy Popcorn Shrimp

Servings: 4
Cooking Time: 10 Minutes
Ingredients:

- 170g shrimp, peeled and diced
- ½ cup breadcrumbs
- Salt and black pepper to taste
- 2 eggs, beaten

Directions:

1. Mix breadcrumbs with black pepper and salt in a bowl.
2. Dip the shrimp pieces in the eggs and coat each with breadcrumbs.
3. Divide the shrimp popcorn into the 2 Air Fryer baskets.
4. Return the air fryer basket 1 to Zone 1, and basket 2 to Zone 2 of the Tefal 2-Basket Air Fryer.
5. Choose the "Air Fry" mode for Zone 1 at 400 degrees F and 6 minutes of cooking time.
6. Select the "MATCH COOK" option to copy the settings for Zone 2.
7. Initiate cooking by pressing the START/PAUSE BUTTON.
8. Serve warm.

Kale Chips

Servings: 4
Cooking Time: 3 Minutes
Ingredients:

- 1 head fresh kale, stems and ribs removed and cut into 4cm pieces
- 1 tablespoon olive oil
- 1 teaspoon soy sauce
- ⅛ teaspoon cayenne pepper
- Pinch of freshly ground black pepper

Directions:

1. In a large bowl, add all the ingredients and mix well.
2. Grease basket of Tefal 2-Basket Air Fryer.
3. Press your chosen zone - "Zone 1" or "Zone 2" and then rotate the knob to select "Air Fry".
4. Set the temperature to 200 degrees C and then set the time for 5 minutes to preheat.
5. After preheating, arrange the kale pieces into the basket of each zone.
6. Slide the basket into the Air Fryer and set the time for 3 minutes.
7. While cooking, toss the kale pieces once halfway through.
8. After cooking time is completed, remove the kale chips and baking pans from Air Fryer.
9. Place the kale chips onto a wire rack to cool for about 10 minutes before serving.

Mexican Jalapeno Poppers

Servings: 8
Cooking Time: 5 Minutes
Ingredients:

- 5 jalapenos, cut in half & remove seeds
- ¼ tsp red pepper flakes, crushed
- 1 tsp onion powder
- 32g salsa
- 113g goat cheese
- 1 tsp garlic powder
- Pepper
- Salt

Directions:

1. In a small bowl, mix goat cheese, salsa, red pepper flakes, onion powder, garlic powder, pepper, and salt.
2. Stuff each jalapeno half with goat cheese mixture.
3. Insert a crisper plate in the Tefal air fryer baskets.
4. Place stuffed peppers in both baskets.
5. Select zone 1 then select "air fry" mode and set the temperature to 360 degrees F for 8 minutes—Press "match" to match zone 2 settings to zone 1. Press "start/stop" to begin.

Cinnamon-apple Crisps

Servings: 4
Cooking Time: 32 Minutes
Ingredients:

- Oil, for spraying
- 2 Red Delicious or Honeycrisp apples
- ¼ teaspoon ground cinnamon, divided

Directions:

1. Line the two air fryer baskets with parchment and spray lightly with oil.
2. Trim the uneven ends off the apples. Using a mandoline slicer on the thinnest setting or a sharp knife, cut the apples into very thin slices. Discard the cores.
3. Place the apple slices in a single layer in the two prepared baskets and sprinkle with the cinnamon.
4. Place two metal air fryer trivets on top of the apples to keep them from flying around while they are cooking.
5. Air fry at 150°C for 16 minutes, flipping every 5 minutes to ensure even cooking.
6. Let cool to room temperature before serving. The crisps will firm up as they cool.

Bacon Wrapped Tater Tots

Servings: 8
Cooking Time: 15 Minutes
Ingredients:

- 8 bacon slices
- 3 tablespoons honey
- ½ tablespoon chipotle chile powder
- 16 frozen tater tots

Directions:

1. Cut the bacon slices in half and wrap each tater tot with a bacon slice.
2. Brush the bacon with honey and drizzle chipotle chile powder over them.
3. Insert a toothpick to seal the bacon.
4. Place the wrapped tots in the air fryer baskets.
5. Return the air fryer basket 1 to Zone 1, and basket 2 to Zone 2 of the Tefal 2-Basket Air Fryer.
6. Choose the "Air Fry" mode for Zone 1 at 350 degrees F and 14 minutes of cooking time.
7. Select the "MATCH COOK" option to copy the settings for Zone 2.
8. Initiate cooking by pressing the START/PAUSE BUTTON.
9. Serve warm.

Fried Pickles

Servings: 4
Cooking Time: 15 Minutes
Ingredients:

- 2 cups sliced dill pickles
- 1 cup flour
- 1 tablespoon garlic powder
- 1 tablespoon Cajun spice
- ½ tablespoon cayenne pepper
- Olive Oil or cooking spray

Directions:

1. Mix together the flour and spices in a bowl.
2. Coat the sliced pickles with the flour mixture.
3. Place a crisper plate in each drawer. Put the pickles in a single layer in each drawer. Insert the drawers into the unit.
4. Select zone 1, then AIR FRY, then set the temperature to 400 degrees F/ 200 degrees C with a 15-minute timer. To match zone 2 settings to zone 1, choose MATCH. To begin, select START/STOP.

Nutrition:

- (Per serving) Calories 161 | Fat 4.1g | Sodium 975mg | Carbs 27.5g | Fiber 2.2g | Sugar 1.5g | Protein 4g

"fried" Ravioli With Zesty Marinara

Servings:6

Cooking Time: 20 Minutes

Ingredients:

- FOR THE RAVIOLI
- ¼ cup all-purpose flour
- 1 large egg
- 1 tablespoon water
- ⅔ cup Italian-style bread crumbs
- 1 pound frozen cheese ravioli, thawed
- Nonstick cooking spray
- FOR THE MARINARA
- 1 (28-ounce) can chunky crushed tomatoes with basil and oregano
- 1 tablespoon unsalted butter
- 2 garlic cloves, minced
- ¼ teaspoon kosher salt
- ¼ teaspoon red pepper flakes

Directions:

1. To prep the ravioli: Set up a breading station with three small shallow bowls. Put the flour in the first bowl. In the second bowl, beat the egg and water. Place the bread crumbs in the third bowl.
2. Bread the ravioli in this order: First dip them into the flour, coating both sides. Then dip into the beaten egg. Finally, coat them in the bread crumbs, gently pressing the crumbs into the ravioli to help them stick.
3. Mist both sides of the ravioli generously with cooking spray.
4. To prep the marinara: In the Zone 2 basket, combine the crushed tomatoes, butter, garlic, salt, and red pepper flakes.
5. To cook the ravioli and sauce: Install a crisper plate in the Zone 1 basket and add the ravioli to the basket. Insert the basket in the unit. Insert the Zone 2 basket in the unit.
6. Select Zone 1, select AIR FRY, set the temperature to 390°F, and set the time to 20 minutes.
7. Select Zone 2, select BAKE, set the temperature to 350°F, and set the time to 15 minutes. Select SMART FINISH.
8. Press START/PAUSE to begin cooking.
9. When the Zone 1 timer reads 7 minutes, press START/PAUSE. Remove the basket and shake to redistribute the ravioli. Reinsert the basket and press START/PAUSE to resume cooking.
10. When cooking is complete, the breading will be crisp and golden brown. Transfer the ravioli to a plate and the marinara to a bowl. Serve hot.

Nutrition:

- (Per serving) Calories: 282; Total fat: 8g; Saturated fat: 3g; Carbohydrates: 39g; Fiber: 4.5g; Protein: 13g; Sodium: 369mg

Onion Pakoras

Servings: 2

Cooking Time: 10 Minutes

Ingredients:

- 2 medium brown or white onions, sliced (475 ml)
- 120 ml chopped fresh coriander
- 2 tablespoons vegetable oil
- 1 tablespoon chickpea flour
- 1 tablespoon rice flour, or 2 tablespoons chickpea flour
- 1 teaspoon ground turmeric
- 1 teaspoon cumin seeds
- 1 teaspoon rock salt
- ½ teaspoon cayenne pepper
- Vegetable oil spray

Directions:

1. In a large bowl, combine the onions, coriander, oil, chickpea flour, rice flour, turmeric, cumin seeds, salt, and cayenne. Stir to combine. Cover and let stand for 30 minutes or up to overnight. Mix well before using.
2. Spray the air fryer baskets generously with vegetable oil spray. Drop the batter in 6 heaping tablespoons into the two baskets. Set the air fryer to 175°C for 8 minutes. Carefully turn the pakoras over and spray with oil spray. Set the air fryer for 2 minutes, or until the batter is cooked through and crisp, checking at 6 minutes for doneness. Serve hot.

Taco-spiced Chickpeas And Black Bean Corn Dip

Servings: 7
Cooking Time: 17 Minutes

Ingredients:

- Taco-Spiced Chickpeas:
- Oil, for spraying
- 1 (439 g) can chickpeas, drained
- 1 teaspoon chilli powder
- ½ teaspoon ground cumin
- ½ teaspoon salt
- ½ teaspoon granulated garlic
- 2 teaspoons lime juice
- Black Bean Corn Dip:
- ½ (425 g) can black beans, drained and rinsed
- ½ (425 g) can corn, drained and rinsed
- 60 ml chunky salsa
- 57 g low-fat soft white cheese
- 60 ml shredded low-fat Cheddar cheese
- ½ teaspoon ground cumin
- ½ teaspoon paprika
- Salt and freshly ground black pepper, to taste

Directions:

1. Make the Taco-Spiced Chickpeas :
2. Line the zone 1 air fryer basket with parchment and spray lightly with oil. Place the chickpeas in the prepared basket.
3. Air fry at 200°C for 17 minutes, shaking or stirring the chickpeas and spraying lightly with oil every 5 to 7 minutes.
4. In a small bowl, mix together the chilli powder, cumin, salt, and garlic.
5. When 2 to 3 minutes of cooking time remain, sprinkle half of the seasoning mix over the chickpeas. Finish cooking.
6. Transfer the chickpeas to a medium bowl and toss with the remaining seasoning mix and the lime juice. Serve immediately.
7. Make the Black Bean Corn Dip :
8. Preheat the air fryer to 165°C.
9. In a medium bowl, mix together the black beans, corn, salsa, soft white cheese, Cheddar cheese, cumin, and paprika. Season with salt and pepper and stir until well combined.
10. Spoon the mixture into a baking dish.
11. Place baking dish in the zone 2 air fryer basket and bake until heated through, about 10 minutes.
12. Serve hot.

Crispy Calamari Rings

Servings: 4
Cooking Time: 10 Minutes

Ingredients:

- 455g calamari rings, patted dry
- 3 tablespoons lemon juice
- 60g plain flour
- 1 teaspoon garlic powder
- 2 egg whites
- 60ml milk
- 220g panko breadcrumbs
- 1½ teaspoon salt
- 1½ teaspoon ground black pepper

Directions:

1. Allow the squid rings to marinade for at least 30 minutes in a bowl with lemon juice. Drain the water in a colander.
2. In a shallow bowl, combine the flour and garlic powder.
3. In a separate bowl, whisk together the egg whites and milk.
4. In a third bowl, combine the panko breadcrumbs, salt, and pepper.
5. Floured first the calamari rings, then dip in the egg mixture, and finally in the panko breadcrumb mixture.
6. Press either "Zone 1" or "Zone 2" and then rotate the knob to select "Air Fry".
7. Set the temperature to 200 degrees C, and then set the time for 5 minutes to preheat.
8. After preheating, spray the Air-Fryer basket with cooking spray and line with parchment paper. Arrange in a single layer and spritz them with cooking spray.
9. Slide the basket into the Air Fryer and set the time for 10 minutes.
10. After cooking time is completed, transfer them onto serving plates and serve.

Crab Cakes

Servings: 4
Cooking Time: 15 Minutes
Ingredients:

- 227g lump crab meat
- 1 red capsicum, chopped
- 3 green onions, chopped
- 3 tablespoons mayonnaise
- 3 tablespoons breadcrumbs
- 2 teaspoons old bay seasoning
- 1 teaspoon lemon juice

Directions:

1. Mix crab meat with capsicum, onions and the rest of the ingredients in a food processor.
2. Make 4 inch crab cakes out of this mixture.
3. Divide the crab cakes into the Tefal 2 Baskets Air Fryer baskets.
4. Return the air fryer basket 1 to Zone 1, and basket 2 to Zone 2 of the Tefal 2-Basket Air Fryer.
5. Choose the "Air Fry" mode for Zone 1 at 370 degrees F and 10 minutes of cooking time.
6. Select the "MATCH COOK" option to copy the settings for Zone 2.
7. Initiate cooking by pressing the START/PAUSE BUTTON.
8. Flip the crab cakes once cooked halfway through.
9. Serve warm.

Cheese Corn Fritters

Servings: 6
Cooking Time: 15 Minutes
Ingredients:

- 1 egg
- 164g corn
- 2 green onions, diced
- 45g flour
- 29g breadcrumbs
- 117g cheddar cheese, shredded
- ½ tsp onion powder
- ½ tsp garlic powder
- 15g sour cream
- Pepper
- Salt

Directions:

1. In a large bowl, add all ingredients and mix until well combined.
2. Insert a crisper plate in the Tefal air fryer baskets.
3. Make patties from the mixture and place them in both baskets.
4. Select zone 1, then select "air fry" mode and set the temperature to 370 degrees F for 12 minutes. Press "match" to match zone 2 settings to zone 1. Press "start/stop" to begin. Turn halfway through.

Dried Apple Chips Dried Banana Chips

Servings:6
Cooking Time: 6 To 10 Hours
Ingredients:

- FOR THE APPLE CHIPS
- ½ teaspoon ground cinnamon
- ¼ teaspoon ground nutmeg
- ⅛ teaspoon ground allspice
- ⅛ teaspoon ground ginger
- 2 Gala apples, cored and cut into ⅛-inch-thick rings
- FOR THE BANANA CHIPS
- 2 firm-ripe bananas, cut into ¼-inch slices

Directions:

1. To prep the apple chips: In a small bowl, mix the cinnamon, nutmeg, allspice, and ginger until combined. Sprinkle the spice mixture over the apple slices.
2. To dehydrate the fruit: Arrange half of the apple slices in a single layer in the Zone 1 basket. It is okay if the edges overlap a bit as they will shrink as they cook. Place a crisper plate on top of the apples. Arrange the remaining apple slices on top of the crisper plate and insert the basket in the unit.
3. Repeat this process with the bananas in the Zone 2 basket and insert the basket in the unit.
4. Select Zone 1, select DEHYDRATE, set the temperature to 135°F, and set the time to 8 hours.
5. Select Zone 2, select DEHYDRATE, set the temperature to 135°F, and set the time to 10 hours. Select SMART FINISH.
6. Press START/PAUSE to begin cooking.
7. When both timers read 2 hours, press START/PAUSE. Remove both baskets and check the fruit for doneness; note that juicier fruit will take longer to dry than fruit that starts out drier. Reinsert the basket and press START/PAUSE to continue cooking if necessary.

Nutrition:

- (Per serving) Calories: 67; Total fat: 0g; Saturated fat: 0g; Carbohydrates: 16g; Fiber: 3g; Protein: 0g; Sodium: 1mg

Cheese Drops

Servings: 8
Cooking Time: 10 Minutes
Ingredients:

- 177 ml plain flour
- ½ teaspoon rock salt
- ¼ teaspoon cayenne pepper
- ¼ teaspoon smoked paprika
- ¼ teaspoon black pepper
- Dash garlic powder (optional)
- 60 ml butter, softened
- 240 ml shredded extra mature Cheddar cheese, at room temperature
- Olive oil spray

Directions:

1. In a small bowl, combine the flour, salt, cayenne, paprika, pepper, and garlic powder, if using. 2. Using a food processor, cream the butter and cheese until smooth. Gently add the seasoned flour and process until the dough is well combined, smooth, and no longer sticky. 3. Divide the dough into 32 equal-size pieces. On a lightly floured surface, roll each piece into a small ball. 4. Spray the two air fryer baskets with oil spray. Arrange the cheese drops in the two baskets. Set the air fryer to 165°C for 10 minutes, or until drops are just starting to brown. Transfer to a wire rack. 5. Cool the cheese drops completely on the wire rack. Store in an airtight container until ready to serve, or up to 1 or 2 days.

Garlic Bread

Servings: 8
Cooking Time: 10 Minutes
Ingredients:

- 60g butter, softened
- 3 tablespoons grated Parmesan cheese
- 2 garlic cloves, minced
- 2 teaspoons minced fresh parsley
- 8 slices of French bread

Directions:

1. Press either "Zone 1" or "Zone 2" and then rotate the knob to select "Bake".
2. Set the temperature to 175 degrees C, and then set the time for 5 minutes to preheat.
3. After preheating, combine the first four ingredients in a small mixing bowl| spread on bread. Arrange bread slices onto basket.
4. Slide the basket into the Air Fryer and set the time for 3 minutes.
5. After cooking time is completed, transfer them onto serving plates and serve.

Shrimp Pirogues

Servings: 8
Cooking Time: 4 To 5 Minutes
Ingredients:

- 340 g small, peeled, and deveined raw shrimp
- 85 g soft white cheese, room temperature
- 2 tablespoons natural yoghurt
- 1 teaspoon lemon juice
- 1 teaspoon dried dill weed, crushed
- Salt, to taste
- 4 small hothouse cucumbers, each approximately 6 inches long

Directions:

1. Pour 4 tablespoons water in bottom of air fryer drawer.
2. Place shrimp in air fryer basket in single layer and air fry at 200°C for 4 to 5 minutes, just until done. Watch carefully because shrimp cooks quickly, and overcooking makes it tough.
3. Chop shrimp into small pieces, no larger than ½ inch. Refrigerate while mixing the remaining ingredients.
4. With a fork, mash and whip the soft white cheese until smooth.
5. Stir in the yoghurt and beat until smooth. Stir in lemon juice, dill weed, and chopped shrimp.
6. Taste for seasoning. If needed, add ¼ to ½ teaspoon salt to suit your taste.
7. Store in refrigerator until serving time.
8. When ready to serve, wash and dry cucumbers and split them lengthwise. Scoop out the seeds and turn cucumbers upside down on paper towels to drain for 10 minutes.
9. Just before filling, wipe centres of cucumbers dry. Spoon the shrimp mixture into the pirogues and cut in half crosswise. Serve immediately.

Healthy Spinach Balls

Servings: 4
Cooking Time: 15 Minutes
Ingredients:

- 1 egg
- 29g breadcrumbs
- ½ medium onion, chopped
- 225g spinach, blanched & chopped
- 1 carrot, peel & grated
- 1 tbsp cornflour
- 1 tbsp nutritional yeast
- 1 tsp garlic, minced
- ½ tsp garlic powder
- Pepper
- Salt

Directions:

1. Add spinach and remaining ingredients into the mixing bowl and mix until well combined.
2. Insert a crisper plate in the Tefal air fryer baskets.
3. Make small balls from the spinach mixture and place them in both baskets.
4. Select zone 1, then select "air fry" mode and set the temperature to 390 degrees F for 10 minutes. Press "match" to match zone 2 settings to zone 1. Press "start/stop" to begin.

Mozzarella Sticks

Servings: 6
Cooking Time: 6 Minutes
Ingredients:

- 150g block Mozzarella cheese or string cheese
- 6 slices of white bread
- 1 large egg
- 1 tablespoon water
- 55g panko breadcrumbs
- 1 tablespoon olive oil

Directions:

1. Remove the crust from the bread. Discard or save for breadcrumbs.
2. Roll the bread into thin slices with a rolling pin.
3. Slice mozzarella into 30 cm x 10 cm -long sticks, nearly the same size as your bread slices.
4. In a small bowl, whisk together the egg and the water.
5. Fill a shallow pie plate halfway with panko.
6. Wrap a bread slice around each mozzarella stick.
7. Brush the egg wash around the edge of the bread and push to seal it. Brush all over the bread outside.
8. Dredge in Panko and push to coat on all sides.
9. Line basket with parchment paper.
10. Press either "Zone 1" or "Zone 2" and then rotate the knob to select "Air Fryer".
11. Set the temperature to 200 degrees C, and then set the time for 5 minutes to preheat.
12. After preheating, arrange sticks into the basket.
13. Slide the basket into the Air Fryer and set the time for 6 minutes.
14. After cooking time is completed, place on a wire rack for a few minutes, then transfer onto serving plates and serve.

Tofu Veggie Meatballs

Servings: 4
Cooking Time: 15 Minutes
Ingredients:

- 122g firm tofu, drained
- 50g breadcrumbs
- 37g bamboo shoots, thinly sliced
- 22g carrots, shredded & steamed
- 1 tsp garlic powder
- 1 ½ tbsp soy sauce
- 2 tbsp cornstarch
- 3 dried shitake mushrooms, soaked & chopped
- Pepper
- Salt

Directions:

1. Add tofu and remaining ingredients into the food processor and process until well combined.
2. Insert a crisper plate in the Tefal air fryer baskets.
3. Make small balls from the tofu mixture and place them in both baskets.
4. Select zone 1, then select "air fry" mode and set the temperature to 380 degrees F for 10 minutes. Press "match" to match zone 2 settings to zone 1. Press "start/stop" to begin. Turn halfway through.

Vegetables And Sides Recipes

Lemon Herb Cauliflower

Servings: 4
Cooking Time: 10 Minutes
Ingredients:

- 384g cauliflower florets
- 1 tsp lemon zest, grated
- 1 tbsp thyme, minced
- 60ml olive oil
- 1 tbsp rosemary, minced
- ¼ tsp red pepper flakes, crushed
- 30ml lemon juice
- 25g parsley, minced
- ½ tsp salt

Directions:

1. In a bowl, toss cauliflower florets with the remaining ingredients until well coated.
2. Insert a crisper plate in the Tefal air fryer baskets.
3. Add cauliflower florets into both baskets.
4. Select zone 1, then select "air fry" mode and set the temperature to 360 degrees F for 10 minutes. Press "match" and "start/stop" to begin.

Nutrition:

- (Per serving) Calories 166 | Fat 14.4g |Sodium 340mg | Carbs 9.5g | Fiber 4.6g | Sugar 3.8g | Protein 3.3g

Garlic-herb Fried Squash

Servings: 4
Cooking Time: 15 Minutes
Ingredients:

- 5 cups halved small pattypan squash (about 1¼ pounds)
- 1 tablespoon olive oil
- 2 garlic cloves, minced
- ½ teaspoon salt
- ¼ teaspoon dried oregano
- ¼ teaspoon dried thyme
- ¼ teaspoon pepper
- 1 tablespoon minced fresh parsley, for serving

Directions:

1. Place the squash in a large bowl.
2. Mix the oil, garlic, salt, oregano, thyme, and pepper| drizzle over the squash. Toss to coat.
3. Place a crisper plate in both drawers. Put the squash in a single layer in each drawer. Insert the drawers into the unit.
4. Select zone 1, then AIR FRY, then set the temperature to 360 degrees F/ 180 degrees C with a 6-minute timer. To match zone 2 settings to zone 1, choose MATCH. To begin, select START/STOP.
5. Remove the squash from the drawers after the timer has finished. Sprinkle with the parsley.

Fried Patty Pan Squash

Servings: 6
Cooking Time: 15 Minutes
Ingredients:

- 5 cups small pattypan squash, halved
- 1 tablespoon olive oil
- 2 garlic cloves, minced
- ½ teaspoon salt
- ¼ teaspoon dried oregano
- ¼ teaspoon dried thyme
- ¼ teaspoon pepper
- 1 tablespoon minced parsley

Directions:

1. Rub the squash with oil, garlic and the rest of the ingredients.
2. Spread the squash in the air fryer baskets.
3. Return the air fryer basket 1 to Zone 1, and basket 2 to Zone 2 of the Tefal 2-Basket Air Fryer.
4. Choose the "Air Fry" mode for Zone 1 at 375 degrees F and 15 minutes of cooking time.
5. Select the "MATCH COOK" option to copy the settings for Zone 2.
6. Initiate cooking by pressing the START/PAUSE BUTTON.
7. Flip the squash once cooked halfway through.
8. Garnish with parsley.
9. Serve warm.

Nutrition:

- (Per serving) Calories 208 | Fat 5g |Sodium 1205mg | Carbs 34.1g | Fiber 7.8g | Sugar 2.5g | Protein 5.9g

Jerk Tofu With Roasted Cabbage

Servings:4
Cooking Time: 20 Minutes
Ingredients:

- FOR THE JERK TOFU
- 1 (14-ounce) package extra-firm tofu, drained
- 1 tablespoon apple cider vinegar
- 1 tablespoon reduced-sodium soy sauce
- 2 tablespoons jerk seasoning
- Juice of 1 lime
- ½ teaspoon kosher salt
- 2 tablespoons olive oil
- FOR THE CABBAGE
- 1 (14-ounce) bag coleslaw mix
- 1 red bell pepper, thinly sliced
- 2 scallions, thinly sliced
- 2 tablespoons water
- 3 garlic cloves, minced
- ¼ teaspoon fresh thyme leaves
- ¼ teaspoon onion powder
- ¼ teaspoon kosher salt
- ¼ teaspoon freshly ground black pepper

Directions:

1. To prep the jerk tofu: Cut the tofu horizontally into 4 slabs.
2. In a shallow dish (big enough to hold the tofu slabs), whisk together the vinegar, soy sauce, jerk seasoning, lime juice, and salt.
3. Place the tofu in the marinade and turn to coat both sides. Cover and marinate for at least 15 minutes (or up to overnight in the refrigerator).
4. To prep the cabbage: In the Zone 2 basket, combine the coleslaw, bell pepper, scallions, water, garlic, thyme, onion powder, salt, and black pepper.
5. To cook the tofu and cabbage: Install a crisper plate in the Zone 1 basket and add the tofu in a single layer. Brush the tofu with the oil and insert the basket in the unit. Insert the Zone 2 basket in the unit.
6. Select Zone 1, select AIR FRY, set the temperature to 390°F, and set the timer to 15 minutes.
7. Select Zone 2, select ROAST, set the temperature to 330°F, and set the timer to 20 minutes. Select SMART FINISH.
8. Press START/PAUSE to begin cooking.
9. When both timers read 5 minutes, press START/PAUSE. Remove the Zone 1 basket and use silicone-tipped tongs to flip the tofu. Reinsert the basket in the unit. Remove the Zone 2 basket and stir the cabbage. Reinsert the basket and press START/PAUSE to resume cooking.
10. When cooking is complete, the tofu will be crispy and browned around the edges and the cabbage soft.
11. Transfer the tofu to four plates and serve with the cabbage on the side.

Nutrition:

- (Per serving) Calories: 220; Total fat: 12g; Saturated fat: 1.5g; Carbohydrates: 21g; Fiber: 5g; Protein: 12g; Sodium: 817mg

Beets With Orange Gremolata And Goat's Cheese

Servings: 12
Cooking Time: 45 Minutes
Ingredients:

- 3 medium fresh golden beets (about 1 pound)
- 3 medium fresh beets (about 1 pound)
- 2 tablespoons lime juice
- 2 tablespoons orange juice
- ½ teaspoon fine sea salt
- 1 tablespoon minced fresh parsley
- 1 tablespoon minced fresh sage
- 1 garlic clove, minced
- 1 teaspoon grated orange zest
- 3 tablespoons crumbled goat's cheese
- 2 tablespoons sunflower kernels

Directions:

1. Scrub the beets and trim the tops by 1 inch.
2. Place the beets on a double thickness of heavy-duty foil . Fold the foil around the beets, sealing tightly.
3. Place a crisper plate in both drawers. Put the beets in a single layer in each drawer. Insert the drawers into the unit.
4. Select zone 1, then AIR FRY, then set the temperature to 360 degrees F/ 180 degrees C with a 45-minute timer. To match zone 2 settings to zone 1, choose MATCH. To begin, select START/STOP.
5. Remove the beets from the drawers after the timer has finished. Peel, halve, and slice them when they're cool enough to handle. Place them in a serving bowl.
6. Toss in the lime juice, orange juice, and salt to coat. Sprinkle the beets with the parsley, sage, garlic, and orange zest. The sunflower kernels and goat's cheese go on top.

Air-fried Radishes

Servings: 6

Cooking Time: 15 Minutes

Ingredients:

- 1020g radishes, quartered
- 3 tablespoons olive oil
- 1 tablespoon fresh oregano, minced
- ¼ teaspoon salt
- ⅛ teaspoon black pepper

Directions:

1. Toss radishes with oil, black pepper, salt and oregano in a bowl.
2. Divide the radishes into the Tefal 2 Baskets Air Fryer baskets.
3. Return the air fryer basket 1 to Zone 1, and basket 2 to Zone 2 of the Tefal 2-Basket Air Fryer.
4. Choose the "Air Fry" mode for Zone 1 at 375 degrees F and 15 minutes of cooking time.
5. Select the "MATCH COOK" option to copy the settings for Zone 2.
6. Initiate cooking by pressing the START/PAUSE BUTTON.
7. Toss the radishes once cooked halfway through.
8. Serve.

Nutrition:

- (Per serving) Calories 270 | Fat 14.6g |Sodium 394mg | Carbs 31.3g | Fiber 7.5g | Sugar 9.7g | Protein 6.4g

Fried Asparagus

Servings: 4

Cooking Time: 6 Minutes

Ingredients:

- ¼ cup mayonnaise
- 4 teaspoons olive oil
- 1½ teaspoons grated lemon zest
- 1 garlic clove, minced
- ½ teaspoon pepper
- ¼ teaspoon seasoned salt
- 1-pound fresh asparagus, trimmed
- 2 tablespoons shredded parmesan cheese
- Lemon wedges (optional)

Directions:

1. In a large bowl, combine the first 6 ingredients.
2. Add the asparagus| toss to coat.
3. Put a crisper plate in both drawers. Put the asparagus in a single layer in each drawer. Top with the parmesan cheese. Place the drawers into the unit.
4. Select zone 1, then AIR FRY, then set the temperature to 375 degrees F/ 190 degrees C with a 6-minute timer. To match zone 2 settings to zone 1, choose MATCH. To begin, select START/STOP.
5. Remove the asparagus from the drawers after the timer has finished.

Delicious Potatoes & Carrots

Servings: 8

Cooking Time: 25 Minutes

Ingredients:

- 453g carrots, sliced
- 2 tsp smoked paprika
- 21g sugar
- 30ml olive oil
- 453g potatoes, diced
- ¼ tsp thyme
- ½ tsp dried oregano
- 1 tsp garlic powder
- Pepper
- Salt

Directions:

1. In a bowl, toss carrots and potatoes with 1 tablespoon of oil.
2. Insert a crisper plate in the Tefal air fryer baskets.
3. Add carrots and potatoes to both baskets.
4. Select zone 1 then select "air fry" mode and set the temperature to 390 degrees F for 15 minutes. Press "match" to match zone 2 settings to zone 1. Press "start/stop" to begin.
5. In a mixing bowl, add cooked potatoes, carrots, smoked paprika, sugar, oil, thyme, oregano, garlic powder, pepper, and salt and toss well.
6. Return carrot and potato mixture into the air fryer basket and cook for 10 minutes more.

Nutrition:

- (Per serving) Calories 101 | Fat 3.6g |Sodium 62mg | Carbs 16.6g | Fiber 3g | Sugar 5.1g | Protein 1.6g

Stuffed Tomatoes

Servings: 2
Cooking Time: 8 Minutes
Ingredients:

- 2 cups brown rice, cooked
- 1 cup tofu, grilled and chopped
- 4 large red tomatoes
- 4 tablespoons basil, chopped
- ¼ tablespoon olive oil
- Salt and black pepper, to taste
- 2 tablespoons lemon juice
- 1 teaspoon red chili powder
- ½ cup Parmesan cheese

Directions:

1. Take a large bowl and mix rice, tofu, basil, olive oil, salt, black pepper, lemon juice, and chili powder.
2. Core the center of the tomatoes.
3. Fill the cavity with the rice mixture.
4. Top them off with the cheese sprinkle.
5. Divide the tomatoes into two air fryer baskets.
6. Turn zone 1 to AIR FRY mode for 8 minutes at 400 degrees F/ 200 degrees C.
7. Select the MATCH button for zone 2.
8. Serve and enjoy.

Sweet Potatoes & Brussels Sprouts

Servings: 8
Cooking Time: 35 Minutes
Ingredients:

- 340g sweet potatoes, cubed
- 30ml olive oil
- 150g onion, cut into pieces
- 352g Brussels sprouts, halved
- Pepper
- Salt
- For glaze:
- 78ml ketchup
- 115ml balsamic vinegar
- 15g mustard
- 29 ml honey

Directions:

1. In a bowl, toss Brussels sprouts, oil, onion, sweet potatoes, pepper, and salt.
2. Insert a crisper plate in the Tefal air fryer baskets.
3. Add Brussels sprouts and sweet potato mixture in both baskets.
4. Select zone 1, then select "air fry" mode and set the temperature to 390 degrees F for 25 minutes. Press "match" to match zone 2 settings to zone 1. Press "start/stop" to begin. Stir halfway through.
5. Meanwhile, add vinegar, ketchup, honey, and mustard to a saucepan and cook over medium heat for 5-10 minutes.
6. Toss cooked sweet potatoes and Brussels sprouts with sauce.

Nutrition:

- (Per serving) Calories 142 | Fat 4.2g |Sodium 147mg | Carbs 25.2g | Fiber 4g | Sugar 8.8g | Protein 2.9g

Pepper Poppers

Servings: 24
Cooking Time: 20 Minutes
Ingredients:

- 8 ounces cream cheese, softened
- ¾ cup shredded cheddar cheese
- ¾ cup shredded Monterey Jack cheese
- 6 bacon strips, cooked and crumbled
- ¼ teaspoon salt
- ¼ teaspoon garlic powder
- ¼ teaspoon chili powder
- ¼ teaspoon smoked paprika
- 1-pound fresh jalapeño peppers, halved lengthwise and deseeded
- ½ cup dry breadcrumbs
- Sour cream, French onion dip, or ranch salad dressing (optional)

Directions:

1. In a large bowl, combine the cheeses, bacon, and seasonings| mix well. Spoon 1½ to 2 tablespoons of the mixture into each pepper half. Roll them in the breadcrumbs.
2. Place a crisper plate in each drawer. Put the prepared peppers in a single layer in each drawer. Insert the drawers into the unit.
3. Select zone 1, then AIR FRY, then set the temperature to 360 degrees F/ 180 degrees C with a 20-minute timer. To match zone 2 settings to zone 1, choose MATCH. To begin, select START/STOP.
4. Remove the peppers from the drawers after the timer has finished.

Herb And Lemon Cauliflower

Servings: 4
Cooking Time: 10 Minutes

Ingredients:

- 1 medium cauliflower, cut into florets (about 6 cups)
- 4 tablespoons olive oil, divided
- ¼ cup minced fresh parsley
- 1 tablespoon minced fresh rosemary
- 1 tablespoon minced fresh thyme
- 1 teaspoon grated lemon zest
- 2 tablespoons lemon juice
- ½ teaspoon salt
- ¼ teaspoon crushed red pepper flakes

Directions:

1. In a large bowl, combine the cauliflower florets and 2 tablespoons olive oil| toss to coat.
2. Put a crisper plate in both drawers, then put the cauliflower in a single layer in each. Insert the drawers into the unit.
3. Select zone 1, then AIR FRY, then set the temperature to 350 degrees F/ 175 degrees C with a 10-minute timer. To match zone 2 settings to zone 1, choose MATCH. To begin, select START/STOP.
4. Remove the cauliflower from the drawers after the timer has finished.
5. In a small bowl, combine the remaining ingredients. Stir in the remaining 2 tablespoons of oil.
6. Transfer the cauliflower to a large bowl and drizzle with the herb mixture. Toss to combine.

Acorn Squash Slices

Servings: 6
Cooking Time: 10 Minutes

Ingredients:

- 2 medium acorn squashes
- ⅔ cup packed brown sugar
- ½ cup butter, melted

Directions:

1. Cut the squash in half, remove the seeds and slice into ½ inch slices.
2. Place the squash slices in the air fryer baskets.
3. Drizzle brown sugar and butter over the squash slices.
4. Return the air fryer basket 1 to Zone 1, and basket 2 to Zone 2 of the Tefal 2-Basket Air Fryer.
5. Choose the "Air Fry" mode for Zone 1 and set the temperature to 350 degrees F and 10 minutes of cooking time.
6. Select the "MATCH COOK" option to copy the settings for Zone 2.
7. Initiate cooking by pressing the START/PAUSE BUTTON.
8. Flip the squash once cooked halfway through.
9. Serve.

Nutrition:

- (Per serving) Calories 206 | Fat 3.4g |Sodium 174mg | Carbs 35g | Fiber 9.4g | Sugar 5.9g | Protein 10.6g

Zucchini With Stuffing

Servings:3
Cooking Time:20

Ingredients:

- 1 cup quinoa, rinsed
- 1 cup black olives
- 6 medium zucchinis, about 2 pounds
- 2 cups cannellini beans, drained
- 1 white onion, chopped
- ¼ cup almonds, chopped
- 4 cloves of garlic, chopped
- 4 tablespoons olive oil
- 1 cup of water
- 2 cups Parmesan cheese, for topping

Directions:

1. First wash the zucchini and cut it lengthwise.
2. Take a skillet and heat oil in it
3. Sauté the onion in olive oil for a few minutes.
4. Then add the quinoa and water and let it cook for 8 minutes with the lid on the top.
5. Transfer the quinoa to a bowl and add all remaining ingredients excluding zucchini and Parmesan cheese.
6. Scoop out the seeds of zucchinis.
7. Fill the cavity of zucchinis with bowl mixture.
8. Top it with a handful of Parmesan cheese.
9. Arrange 4 zucchinis in both air fryer baskets.
10. Select zone1 basket at AIR FRY for 20 minutes and adjusting the temperature to 390 degrees F.
11. Use the Match button to select the same setting for zone 2.
12. Serve and enjoy.

Nutrition:

- (Per serving) Calories 1171| Fat 48.6g| Sodium 1747mg | Carbs 132.4g | Fiber 42.1g | Sugar 11.5g | Protein 65.7g

Lime Glazed Tofu

Servings: 6
Cooking Time: 14 Minutes

Ingredients:

- ⅔ cup coconut aminos

- 2 (14-oz) packages extra-firm, water-packed tofu, drained
- 6 tablespoons toasted sesame oil
- ⅔ cup lime juice

Directions:

1. Pat dry the tofu bars and slice into half-inch cubes.
2. Toss all the remaining ingredients in a small bowl.
3. Marinate for 4 hours in the refrigerator. Drain off the excess water.
4. Divide the tofu cubes in the two crisper plates.
5. Return the crisper plates to the Tefal Dual Zone Air Fryer.
6. Choose the Air Fry mode for Zone 1 and set the temperature to 400 degrees F/ 200 degrees C and the time to 14 minutes.
7. Select the "MATCH" button to copy the settings for Zone 2.
8. Initiate cooking by pressing the START/STOP button.
9. Toss the tofu once cooked halfway through, then resume cooking. 10. Serve warm.

Potatoes & Beans

Servings: 4
Cooking Time: 25 Minutes

Ingredients:

- 453g potatoes, cut into pieces
- 15ml olive oil
- 1 tsp garlic powder
- 160g green beans, trimmed
- Pepper
- Salt

Directions:

1. In a bowl, toss green beans, garlic powder, potatoes, oil, pepper, and salt.
2. Insert a crisper plate in the Tefal air fryer baskets.
3. Add green beans and potato mixture to both baskets.
4. Select zone 1 then select "air fry" mode and set the temperature to 380 degrees F for 25 minutes. Press "match" to match zone 2 settings to zone 1. Press "start/stop" to begin. Stir halfway through.

Nutrition:

- (Per serving) Calories 128 | Fat 3.7g |Sodium 49mg | Carbs 22.4g | Fiber 4.7g | Sugar 2.3g | Protein 3.1g

Falafel

Servings: 6
Cooking Time: 14 Minutes

Ingredients:

- 1 (15.5-oz) can chickpeas, rinsed and drained
- 1 small yellow onion, cut into quarters
- 3 garlic cloves, chopped
- ⅓ cup parsley, chopped
- ⅓ cup cilantro, chopped
- ⅓ cup scallions, chopped
- 1 teaspoon cumin
- ½ teaspoons salt
- ⅛ teaspoons crushed red pepper flakes
- 1 teaspoon baking powder
- 4 tablespoons all-purpose flour
- Olive oil spray

Directions:

1. Dry the chickpeas on paper towels.
2. Add onions and garlic to a food processor and chop them.
3. Add the parsley, salt, cilantro, scallions, cumin, and red pepper flakes.
4. Press the pulse button for 60 seconds, then toss in chickpeas and blend for 3 times until it makes a chunky paste.
5. Stir in baking powder and flour and mix well.
6. Transfer the falafel mixture to a bowl and cover to refrigerate for 3 hours.
7. Make 12 balls out of the falafel mixture.
8. Place 6 falafels in each of the crisper plate and spray them with oil.
9. Return the crisper plate to the Tefal Dual Zone Air Fryer.
10. Choose the Air Fry mode for Zone 1 and set the temperature to 350 degrees F/ 175 degrees C and the time to 14 minutes.
11. Select the "MATCH" button to copy the settings for Zone 2.
12. Initiate cooking by pressing the START/STOP button.
13. Toss the falafel once cooked halfway through, and resume cooking.
14. Serve warm.

Garlic Herbed Baked Potatoes

Servings: 4
Cooking Time: 45 Minutes

Ingredients:

- 4 large baking potatoes
- Salt and black pepper, to taste
- 2 teaspoons avocado oil
- Cheese
- 2 cups sour cream
- 1 teaspoon garlic clove, minced
- 1 teaspoon fresh dill
- 2 teaspoons chopped chives
- Salt and black pepper, to taste
- 2 teaspoons Worcestershire sauce

Directions:

1. Pierce the skin of the potatoes with a fork.
2. Season the potatoes with olive oil, salt, and black pepper.
3. Divide the potatoes into the air fryer baskets.
4. Now press 1 for zone 1 and set it to AIR FRY mode at 350 degrees F/ 175 degrees C, for 45 minutes.
5. Select the MATCH button for zone 2.
6. Meanwhile, take a bowl and mix all the cheese ingredients together.
7. Once the cooking cycle is complete, take out the potatoes and make a slit in-between each one.
8. Add the cheese mixture in the cavity and serve it hot.

Mushroom Roll-ups

Servings: 10
Cooking Time: 10 Minutes

Ingredients:

- 2 tablespoons extra virgin olive oil
- 8 ounces large portobello mushrooms (gills discarded), finely chopped
- 1 teaspoon dried oregano
- 1 teaspoon dried thyme
- ½ teaspoon crushed red pepper flakes
- ¼ teaspoon salt
- 8 ounces cream cheese, softened
- 4 ounces whole-milk ricotta cheese
- 10 flour tortillas (8-inch)
- Cooking spray
- Chutney, for serving (optional)

Directions:

1. Heat the oil in a pan over medium heat. Add the mushrooms and cook for 4 minutes. Sauté until the mushrooms are browned, about 4-6 minutes, with the oregano, thyme, pepper flakes, and salt. Cool.
2. Combine the cheeses in a mixing bowl| fold in the mushrooms until thoroughly combined.
3. On the bottom center of each tortilla, spread 3 tablespoons of the mushroom mixture. Tightly roll up each tortilla and secure with toothpicks.
4. Place a crisper plate in each drawer. Put the roll-ups in a single layer in each. Insert the drawers into the unit.
5. Select zone 1, then AIR FRY, then set the temperature to 400 degrees F/ 200 degrees C with a 10-minute timer. To match zone 2 settings to zone 1, choose MATCH. To begin, select START/STOP.
6. Remove the roll-ups from the drawers after the timer has finished. When they have cooled enough to handle, discard the toothpicks.
7. Serve and enjoy!

Air Fryer Vegetables

Servings: 2
Cooking Time: 15 Minutes

Ingredients:

- 1 courgette, diced
- 2 capsicums, diced
- 1 head broccoli, diced
- 1 red onion, diced
- Marinade
- 1 teaspoon smoked paprika
- 1 teaspoon garlic granules
- 1 teaspoon Herb de Provence
- Salt and black pepper, to taste
- 1½ tablespoon olive oil
- 2 tablespoons lemon juice

Directions:

1. Toss the veggies with the rest of the marinade ingredients in a bowl.
2. Spread the veggies in the air fryer baskets.
3. Return the air fryer basket 1 to Zone 1, and basket 2 to Zone 2 of the Tefal 2-Basket Air Fryer.
4. Choose the "Air Fry" mode for Zone 1 at 400 degrees F and 15 minutes of cooking time.
5. Select the "MATCH COOK" option to copy the settings for Zone 2.
6. Initiate cooking by pressing the START/PAUSE BUTTON.
7. Toss the veggies once cooked half way through.
8. Serve warm.

Nutrition:

- (Per serving) Calories 166 | Fat 3.2g |Sodium 437mg | Carbs 28.8g | Fiber 1.8g | Sugar 2.7g | Protein 5.8g

Breakfast Recipes

Cinnamon Toast

Servings: 6
Cooking Time: 5 Minutes
Ingredients:

- 12 slices bread
- 115g butter, at room temperature
- 100g white sugar
- 1½ teaspoons ground cinnamon
- 1½ teaspoons pure vanilla extract
- 1 pinch of salt

Directions:

1. Softened butter is mashed with a fork or the back of a spoon, and then sugar, cinnamon, vanilla, and salt are added.
2. Stir everything together thoroughly.
3. Spread one-sixth of the mixture onto each slice of bread, covering the entire surface.
4. Press your chosen zone - "Zone 1" or "Zone 2" and then rotate the knob to select "Air Fryer".
5. Set the temperature to 200 degrees C, and then set the time for 3 minutes to preheat.
6. After preheating, arrange bread into the basket of each zone.
7. Slide the basket into the Air Fryer and set the time for 5 minutes.
8. After cooking time is completed, remove both baskets from Air Fryer.
9. Cut bread slices diagonally and serve.

Spinach And Swiss Frittata With Mushrooms

Servings: 4
Cooking Time: 20 Minutes
Ingredients:

- Olive oil cooking spray
- 8 large eggs
- ½ teaspoon salt
- ½ teaspoon black pepper
- 1 garlic clove, minced
- 475 ml fresh baby spinach
- 110 g baby mushrooms, sliced
- 1 shallot, diced
- 120 ml shredded Swiss cheese, divided
- Hot sauce, for serving (optional)

Directions:

1. Lightly coat the inside of a 6-inch round cake pan with olive oil cooking spray. In a large bowl, beat the eggs, salt, pepper, and garlic for 1 to 2 minutes, or until well combined.
2. Fold in the spinach, mushrooms, shallot, and 60 ml the Swiss cheese. Pour the egg mixture into the prepared cake pan, and sprinkle the remaining 60 ml Swiss over the top. Place into the zone 1 drawer.
3. Select Bake button and adjust temperature to 180°C, set time to 18 to 20 minutes and press Start. After the end, remove from the air fryer and allow to cool for 5 minutes. Drizzle with hot sauce before serving.

Pepper Egg Cups

Servings: 4
Cooking Time: 18 Minutes.
Ingredients:

- 2 halved bell pepper, seeds removed
- 4 eggs
- 1 teaspoon olive oil
- 1 pinch salt and black pepper
- 1 pinch sriracha flakes

Directions:

1. Slice the bell peppers in half, lengthwise, and remove their seeds and the inner portion to get a cup-like shape.
2. Rub olive oil on the edges of the bell peppers.
3. Place them in the two crisper plates with their cut side up and crack 1 egg in each half of bell pepper.
4. Drizzle salt, black pepper, and sriracha flakes on top of the eggs.
5. Return the crisper plates to the Tefal Dual Zone Air Fryer.
6. Choose the Air Fry mode for Zone 1 and set the temperature to 390 degrees F and the time to 18 minutes.
7. Select the "MATCH" button to copy the settings for Zone 2.
8. Initiate cooking by pressing the START/STOP button.
9. Serve warm and fresh.

Nutrition:

- (Per serving) Calories 183 | Fat 15g |Sodium 402mg | Carbs 2.5g | Fiber 0.4g | Sugar 1.1g | Protein 10g

Healthy Oatmeal Muffins

Servings: 6
Cooking Time: 17 Minutes
Ingredients:

- 1 egg
- ¼ tsp ground ginger
- 1 tsp ground cinnamon
- ½ tsp baking soda
- ½ tsp baking powder
- 55g brown sugar
- ½ tsp vanilla
- 2 tbsp butter, melted
- 125g applesauce
- 61ml milk
- 68gm whole wheat flour
- 100gm quick oats
- Pinch of salt

Directions:

1. In a mixing bowl, mix together all dry the ingredients.
2. In a separate bowl, add the remaining ingredients and mix well.
3. Add the dry ingredients mixture into the wet mixture and mix until well combined.
4. Pour the batter into the silicone muffin moulds.
5. Insert a crisper plate in the Tefal air fryer baskets.
6. Place muffin moulds in both baskets.
7. Select zone 1 then select "bake" mode and set the temperature to 390 degrees F for 17 minutes. Press "start/stop" to begin.

Nutrition:

- (Per serving) Calories 173 | Fat 5.8g |Sodium 177mg | Carbs 26.6g | Fiber 2.1g | Sugar 8.7g | Protein 4.2g

Bacon-and-eggs Avocado And Simple Scotch Eggs

Servings: 5
Cooking Time: 25 Minutes
Ingredients:

- Bacon-and-Eggs Avocado:
- 1 large egg
- 1 avocado, halved, peeled, and pitted
- 2 slices bacon
- Fresh parsley, for serving (optional)
- Sea salt flakes, for garnish (optional)
- Simple Scotch Eggs:
- 4 large hard boiled eggs
- 1 (340 g) package pork sausage meat
- 8 slices thick-cut bacon
- 4 wooden toothpicks, soaked in water for at least 30 minutes

Directions:

1. Make the Bacon-and-Eggs Avocado :
2. 1. Spray the zone 1 air fryer basket with avocado oil. Preheat the air fryer to 160°C. Fill a small bowl with cool water. Soft-boil the egg: Place the egg in the zone 1 air fryer basket. Air fry for 6 minutes for a soft yolk or 7 minutes for a cooked yolk. Transfer the egg to the bowl of cool water and let sit for 2 minutes. Peel and set aside. 3. Use a spoon to carve out extra space in the center of the avocado halves until the cavities are big enough to fit the soft-boiled egg. Place the soft-boiled egg in the center of one half of the avocado and replace the other half of the avocado on top, so the avocado appears whole on the outside. 4. Starting at one end of the avocado, wrap the bacon around the avocado to completely cover it. Use toothpicks to hold the bacon in place. 5. Place the bacon-wrapped avocado in the zone 1 air fryer basket and air fry for 5 minutes. Flip the avocado over and air fry for another 5 minutes, or until the bacon is cooked to your liking. Serve on a bed of fresh parsley, if desired, and sprinkle with salt flakes, if desired. 6. Best served fresh. Store extras in an airtight container in the fridge for up to 4 days. Reheat in a preheated 160°C air fryer for 4 minutes, or until heated through.
3. Make the Simple Scotch Eggs :
4. Slice the sausage meat into four parts and place each part into a large circle.
5. Put an egg into each circle and wrap it in the sausage. Put in the refrigerator for 1 hour.
6. Preheat the air fryer to 235°C.
7. Make a cross with two pieces of thick-cut bacon. Put a wrapped egg in the center, fold the bacon over top of the egg, and secure with a toothpick.
8. Air fry in the preheated zone 2 air fryer basket for 25 minutes.
9. Serve immediately.

Double-dipped Mini Cinnamon Biscuits

Servings: 8 Biscuits
Cooking Time: 13 Minutes
Ingredients:

- 475 ml blanched almond flour
- 120 ml liquid or powdered sweetener
- 1 teaspoon baking powder
- ½ teaspoon fine sea salt
- 60 ml plus 2 tablespoons (¾ stick) very cold unsalted butter
- 60 ml unsweetened, unflavoured almond milk
- 1 large egg
- 1 teaspoon vanilla extract
- 3 teaspoons ground cinnamon
- Glaze:
- 120 ml powdered sweetener
- 60 ml double cream or unsweetened, unflavoured almond milk

Directions:

1. Preheat the air fryer to 175°C. Line a pie pan that fits into your air fryer with parchment paper. 2. In a medium-sized bowl, mix together the almond flour, sweetener , baking powder, and salt. Cut the butter into ½-inch squares, then use a hand mixer to work the butter into the dry ingredients. When you are done, the mixture should still have chunks of butter. 3. In a small bowl, whisk together the almond milk, egg, and vanilla extract until blended. Using a fork, stir the wet ingredients into the dry ingredients until large clumps form. Add the cinnamon and use your hands to swirl it into the dough. 4. Form the dough into sixteen 1-inch balls and place them on the prepared pan, spacing them about ½ inch apart. Bake in the zone 1 air fryer basket until golden, 10 to 13 minutes. Remove from the air fryer and let cool on the pan for at least 5 minutes. 5. While the biscuits bake, make the glaze: Place the powdered sweetener in a small bowl and slowly stir in the heavy cream with a fork. 6. When the biscuits have cooled somewhat, dip the tops into the glaze, allow it to dry a bit, and then dip again for a thick glaze. 7. Serve warm or at room temperature. Store unglazed biscuits in an airtight container in the refrigerator for up to 3 days or in the freezer for up to a month. Reheat in a preheated 175°C air fryer for 5 minutes, or until warmed through, and dip in the glaze as instructed above.

Bacon, Cheese, And Avocado Melt & Cheesy Scrambled Eggs

Servings: 4
Cooking Time: 9 Minutes
Ingredients:

- Bacon, Cheese, and Avocado Melt:
- 1 avocado
- 4 slices cooked bacon, chopped
- 2 tablespoons salsa
- 1 tablespoon double cream
- 60 ml shredded Cheddar cheese
- Cheesy Scrambled Eggs:
- 1 teaspoon unsalted butter
- 2 large eggs
- 2 tablespoons milk
- 2 tablespoons shredded Cheddar cheese
- Salt and freshly ground black pepper, to taste

Directions:

1. Make the Bacon, Cheese, and Avocado Melt :
2. Preheat the zone 1 air fryer drawer to 204°C.
3. Slice the avocado in half lengthwise and remove the stone. To ensure the avocado halves do not roll in the drawer, slice a thin piece of skin off the base.
4. In a small bowl, combine the bacon, salsa, and cream. Divide the mixture between the avocado halves and top with the cheese.
5. Place the avocado halves in the zone 1 air fryer drawer and air fry for 3 to 5 minutes until the cheese has melted and begins to brown. Serve warm.
6. Make the Cheesy Scrambled Eggs :
7. Preheat the zone 2 air fryer drawer to 150°C. Place the butter in a baking pan and cook for 1 to 2 minutes, until melted.
8. In a small bowl, whisk together the eggs, milk, and cheese. Season with salt and black pepper. Transfer the mixture to the pan.
9. Cook for 3 minutes. Stir the eggs and push them toward the center of the pan.
10. Cook for another 2 minutes, then stir again. Cook for another 2 minutes, until the eggs are just cooked. Serve warm.

Cinnamon Rolls

Servings: 12 Rolls
Cooking Time: 20 Minutes

Ingredients:

- 600 ml shredded Mozzarella cheese
- 60 g cream cheese, softened
- 235 ml blanched finely ground almond flour
- ½ teaspoon vanilla extract
- 120 ml icing sugar-style sweetener
- 1 tablespoon ground cinnamon

Directions:

1. In a large microwave-safe bowl, combine Mozzarella cheese, cream cheese, and flour. Microwave the mixture on high 90 seconds until cheese is melted.
2. Add vanilla extract and sweetener, and mix 2 minutes until a dough forms.
3. Once the dough is cool enough to work with your hands, about 2 minutes, spread it out into a 12 × 4-inch rectangle on ungreased parchment paper. Evenly sprinkle dough with cinnamon.
4. Starting at the long side of the dough, roll lengthwise to form a log. Slice the log into twelve even pieces.
5. Divide rolls between two ungreased round nonstick baking dishes. Place the dishes into the two air fryer drawers. Adjust the temperature to 192°C and bake for 10 minutes.
6. Cinnamon rolls will be done when golden around the edges and mostly firm. Allow rolls to cool in dishes 10 minutes before serving.

Jalapeño Popper Egg Cups And Cheddar Soufflés

Servings: 6
Cooking Time: 12 Minutes

Ingredients:

- Jalapeño Popper Egg Cups:
- 4 large eggs
- 60 ml chopped pickled jalapeños
- 60 g full-fat cream cheese
- 120 ml shredded sharp Cheddar cheese
- Cheddar Soufflés:
- 3 large eggs, whites and yolks separated
- ¼ teaspoon cream of tartar
- 120 ml shredded sharp Cheddar cheese
- 85 g cream cheese, softened

Directions:

1. Make the Jalapeño Popper Egg Cups :
2. In a medium bowl, beat the eggs, then pour into four silicone muffin cups.
3. In a large microwave-safe bowl, place jalapeños, cream cheese, and Cheddar. Microwave for 30 seconds and stir. Take a spoonful, approximately ¼ of the mixture, and place it in the center of one of the egg cups. Repeat with remaining mixture.
4. Place egg cups into the zone 1 air fryer drawer.
5. Adjust the temperature to 160°C and bake for 10 minutes.
6. Serve warm.
7. Make the Cheddar Soufflés :
8. In a large bowl, beat egg whites together with cream of tartar until soft peaks form, about 2 minutes.
9. In a separate medium bowl, beat egg yolks, Cheddar, and cream cheese together until frothy, about 1 minute. Add egg yolk mixture to whites, gently folding until combined.
10. Pour mixture evenly into four ramekins greased with cooking spray. Place ramekins into the zone 2 air fryer drawer. Adjust the temperature to 176°C and bake for 12 minutes. Eggs will be browned on the top and firm in the center when done. Serve warm.

Bacon And Spinach Egg Muffins

Servings: 6
Cooking Time: 12 To 14 Minutes

Ingredients:

- 6 large eggs
- 60 ml double (whipping) cream
- ½ teaspoon sea salt
- ¼ teaspoon freshly ground black pepper
- ¼ teaspoon cayenne pepper (optional)
- 180 ml frozen chopped spinach, thawed and drained
- 4 strips cooked bacon, crumbled
- 60 g shredded Cheddar cheese

Directions:

1. In a large bowl , whisk together the eggs, double cream, salt, black pepper, and cayenne pepper .
2. Divide the spinach and bacon among 6 silicone muffin cups. Place the muffin cups in the zone 1 air fryer drawer.
3. Divide the egg mixture among the muffin cups. Top with the cheese.
4. Set the temperature to 150°C. Bake for 12 to 14 minutes, until the eggs are set and cooked through.

Wholemeal Banana-walnut Bread

Servings: 6
Cooking Time: 23 Minutes

Ingredients:

- Olive oil cooking spray
- 2 ripe medium bananas
- 1 large egg
- 60 ml non-fat plain Greek yoghurt
- 60 ml olive oil
- ½ teaspoon vanilla extract
- 2 tablespoons honey
- 235 ml wholemeal flour
- ¼ teaspoon salt
- ¼ teaspoon baking soda
- ½ teaspoon ground cinnamon
- 60 ml chopped walnuts

Directions:

1. Lightly coat the inside of two 5 ½-by-3-inch loaf pans with olive oil cooking spray.
2. In a large bowl, mash the bananas with a fork. Add the egg, yoghurt, olive oil, vanilla, and honey. Mix until well combined and mostly smooth. Sift the wholemeal flour, salt, baking soda, and cinnamon into the wet mixture, then stir until just combined. Do not overmix. Gently fold in the walnuts. Pour into the prepared loaf pans and spread to distribute evenly.
3. Place a loaf pan in the zone 1 drawer and another pan into zone 2 drawer. In zone 1, select Bake button and adjust temperature to 180°C, set time to 20 to 23 minutes. In zone 2, select Match Cook and press Start.
4. Remove until golden brown on top and a toothpick inserted into the center comes out clean. Allow to cool for 5 minutes before serving.

Breakfast Frittata

Servings: 4
Cooking Time: 12 Minutes

Ingredients:

- 4 eggs
- 4 tablespoons milk
- 35g cheddar cheese grated
- 50g feta crumbled
- 1 tomato, deseeded and chopped
- 15g spinach chopped
- 1 tablespoon fresh herbs, chopped
- 2 spring onion chopped
- Salt and black pepper, to taste
- ½ teaspoon olive oil

Directions:

1. Beat eggs with milk in a bowl and stir in the rest of the ingredients.
2. Grease two small-sized springform pans and line them with parchment paper.
3. Divide the egg mixture into the pans and place one in each air fryer basket.
4. Return the air fryer basket 1 to Zone 1, and basket 2 to Zone 2 of the Tefal 2-Basket Air Fryer.
5. Choose the "Air Fry" mode for Zone 1 at 350 degrees F and 12 minutes of cooking time.
6. Select the "MATCH COOK" option to copy the settings for Zone 2.
7. Initiate cooking by pressing the START/PAUSE BUTTON.
8. Serve warm.

Nutrition:

- (Per serving) Calories 273 | Fat 22g |Sodium 517mg | Carbs 3.3g | Fiber 0.2g | Sugar 1.4g | Protein 16.1g

Bacon And Egg Omelet

Servings:2
Cooking Time:10

Ingredients:

- 2 eggs, whisked
- ½ teaspoon of chopped tomatoes
- Sea Salt and black pepper, to taste
- 2 teaspoons of almond milk
- 1 teaspoon of cilantro, chopped
- 1 small green chili, chopped
- 4 slices of bacon

Directions:

1. Take a bowl and whisk eggs in it.
2. Then add green chili salt, black pepper, cilantro, almond milk, and chopped tomatoes.
3. Oil greases the ramekins.
4. Pour this into ramekins.
5. Put the bacon in the zone 1 basket and ramekins in zone 2 basket of the Tefal 2-Basket Air Fryer.
6. Now for zone 1, set it to AIR FRY mode at 400 degrees F for 10 minutes
7. And for zone 2, set it 350 degrees for 10 minutes in AIR FRY mode.
8. Press the Smart finish button and press start, it will finish both at the same time.
9. Once done, serve and enjoy.

Nutrition:

- (Per serving) Calories 285| Fat 21.5g| Sodium1000 mg | Carbs 2.2g | Fiber 0.1g| Sugar1 g | Protein 19.7g

Donuts

Servings: 6

Cooking Time: 15 Minutes

Ingredients:

- 1 cup granulated sugar
- 2 tablespoons ground cinnamon
- 1 can refrigerated flaky buttermilk biscuits
- ¼ cup unsalted butter, melted

Directions:

1. Combine the sugar and cinnamon in a small shallow bowl and set aside.
2. Remove the biscuits from the can and put them on a chopping board, separated. Cut holes in the center of each biscuit with a 1-inch round biscuit cutter (or a similarly sized bottle cap).
3. Place a crisper plate in each drawer. In each drawer, place 4 biscuits in a single layer. Insert the drawers into the unit.
4. Select zone 1, then AIR FRY, then set the temperature to 360 degrees F/ 180 degrees C with a 10-minute timer. To match zone 2 settings to zone 1, choose MATCH. To begin cooking, select START/STOP.
5. Remove the donuts from the drawers after the timer has finished.

Nutrition:

- (Per serving) Calories 223 | Fat 8g | Sodium 150mg | Carbs 40g | Fiber 1.4g | Sugar 34.2g | Protein 0.8g

Bagels

Servings: 8

Cooking Time: 15 Minutes

Ingredients:

- 2 cups self-rising flour
- 2 cups non-fat plain Greek yogurt
- 2 beaten eggs for egg wash (optional)
- ½ cup sesame seeds (optional)

Directions:

1. In a medium mixing bowl, combine the self-rising flour and Greek yogurt using a wooden spoon.
2. Knead the dough for about 5 minutes on a lightly floured board.
3. Divide the dough into four equal pieces and roll each into a thin rope, securing the ends to form a bagel shape.
4. Install a crisper plate in both drawers. Place 4 bagels in a single layer in each drawer. Insert the drawers into the unit.
5. Select zone 1, select AIR FRY, set temperature to 360 degrees F/ 180 degrees C, and set time to 15 minutes. Select MATCH to match zone 2 settings to zone 1. Select START/STOP to begin.
6. Once the timer has finished, remove the bagels from the units.
7. Serve and enjoy!

Nutrition:

- (Per serving) Calories 202 | Fat 4.5g | Sodium 55mg | Carbs 31.3g | Fiber 2.7g | Sugar 4.7g | Protein 8.7g

Crispy Hash Browns

Servings: 4

Cooking Time: 13 Minutes.

Ingredients:

- 3 russet potatoes
- ¼ cup chopped green peppers
- ¼ cup chopped red peppers
- ¼ cup chopped onions
- 2 garlic cloves chopped
- 1 teaspoon paprika
- Salt and black pepper, to taste
- 2 teaspoons olive oil

Directions:

1. Peel and grate all the potatoes with the help of a cheese grater.
2. Add potato shreds to a bowl filled with cold water and leave it soaked for 25 minutes.
3. Drain the water and place the potato shreds on a plate lined with a paper towel.
4. Transfer the shreds to a dry bowl and add olive oil, paprika, garlic, and black pepper.
5. Make four flat patties out of the potato mixture and place two into each of the crisper plate.
6. Return the crisper plate to the Tefal Dual Zone Air Fryer.
7. Choose the Air Fry mode for Zone 1 and set the temperature to 390 degrees F and set the time to 13 minutes.
8. Select the "MATCH" button to copy the settings for Zone 2.
9. Initiate cooking by pressing the START/STOP button.
10. Flip the potato hash browns once cooked halfway through, then resume cooking.
11. Once done, serve warm.

Nutrition:

- (Per serving) Calories 190 | Fat 18g |Sodium 150mg | Carbs 0.6g | Fiber 0.4g | Sugar 0.4g | Protein 7.2g

Honey-apricot Granola With Greek Yoghurt

Servings: 6
Cooking Time: 30 Minutes

Ingredients:

- 235 ml rolled oats
- 60 ml dried apricots, diced
- 60 ml almond slivers
- 60 ml walnuts, chopped
- 60 ml pumpkin seeds
- 60 to 80 ml honey, plus more for drizzling
- 1 tablespoon olive oil
- 1 teaspoon ground cinnamon
- ¼ teaspoon ground nutmeg
- ¼ teaspoon salt
- 2 tablespoons sugar-free dark chocolate chips (optional)
- 700 ml fat-free plain Greek yoghurt

Directions:

1. Line the zone 1 and zone 2 drawer with two parchment papers. In a large bowl, combine the oats, apricots, almonds, walnuts, pumpkin seeds, honey, olive oil, cinnamon, nutmeg, and salt, mixing so that the honey, oil, and spices are well distributed. Pour the mixture onto the parchment papers and spread it into an even layer.
2. Bake at 130°C for 10 minutes, then shake or stir and spread back out into an even layer. Continue baking for 10 minutes more, then repeat the process of shaking or stirring the mixture.
3. Bake for an additional 10 minutes before removing from the air fryer. Allow the granola to cool completely before stirring in the chocolate chips and pouring into an airtight container for storage. For each serving, top 120 ml Greek yoghurt with 80 ml granola and a drizzle of honey, if needed.

Banana Muffins

Servings: 10
Cooking Time: 15 Minutes

Ingredients:

- 2 very ripe bananas
- ⅓ cup olive oil
- 1 egg
- ½ cup brown sugar
- 1 teaspoon vanilla extract
- 1 teaspoon cinnamon
- ¾ cup self-rising flour

Directions:

1. In a large mixing bowl, mash the bananas, then add the egg, brown sugar, olive oil, and vanilla. To blend, stir everything together thoroughly.
2. Fold in the flour and cinnamon until everything is just blended.
3. Fill muffin molds evenly with the mixture (silicone or paper).
4. Install a crisper plate in both drawers. Place the muffin molds in a single layer in each drawer. Insert the drawers into the unit.
5. Select zone 1, select AIR FRY, set temperature to 360 degrees F/ 180 degrees C, and set time to 15 minutes. Select MATCH to match zone 2 settings to zone 1. Select START/STOP to begin.
6. Once the timer has finished, remove the muffins from the drawers.
7. Serve and enjoy!

Nutrition:

- (Per serving) Calories 148 | Fat 7.3g | Sodium 9mg | Carbs 19.8g | Fiber 1g | Sugar 10g | Protein 1.8g

Honey Banana Oatmeal

Servings: 4
Cooking Time: 8 Minutes

Ingredients:

- 2 eggs
- 2 tbsp honey
- 1 tsp vanilla
- 45g quick oats
- 73ml milk
- 30g Greek yoghurt
- 219g banana, mashed

Directions:

1. In a bowl, mix eggs, milk, yoghurt, honey, vanilla, oats, and mashed banana until well combined.
2. Pour batter into the four greased ramekins.
3. Insert a crisper plate in the Tefal air fryer baskets.
4. Place ramekins in both baskets.
5. Select zone 1 then select "air fry" mode and set the temperature to 390 degrees F for 8 minutes. Press "match" to match zone 2 settings to zone 1. Press "start/stop" to begin.

Nutrition:

- (Per serving) Calories 228 | Fat 4.6g |Sodium 42mg | Carbs 40.4g | Fiber 4.2g | Sugar 16.1g | Protein 7.7g

Baked Mushroom And Mozzarella Frittata With Breakfast Potatoes

Servings:4

Cooking Time: 35 Minutes

Ingredients:

- FOR THE FRITTATA
- 8 large eggs
- ⅓ cup whole milk
- 1 teaspoon kosher salt
- ½ teaspoon freshly ground black pepper
- 1 cup sliced cremini mushrooms (about 2 ounces)
- 1 teaspoon olive oil
- 2 ounces part-skim mozzarella cheese, cut into ½-inch cubes
- FOR THE POTATOES
- 2 russet potatoes, cut into ½-inch cubes
- 1 tablespoon olive oil
- ½ teaspoon garlic powder
- ¼ teaspoon kosher salt
- ¼ teaspoon freshly ground black pepper

Directions:

1. To prep the frittata: In a large bowl, whisk together the eggs, milk, salt, and pepper. Stir in the mushrooms.
2. To prep the potatoes: In a large bowl, combine the potatoes, olive oil, garlic powder, salt, and black pepper.
3. To cook the frittata and potatoes: Brush the bottom of the Zone 1 basket with 1 teaspoon of olive oil. Add the egg mixture to the basket, top with the mozzarella cubes, and insert the basket in the unit. Install a crisper plate in the Zone 2 basket. Place the potatoes in the basket and insert the basket in the unit.
4. Select Zone 1, select BAKE, set the temperature to 350°F, and set the time to 30 minutes.
5. Select Zone 2, select AIR FRY, set the temperature to 400°F, and set the time to 35 minutes. Select SMART FINISH.
6. Press START/PAUSE to begin cooking.
7. When the Zone 2 timer reads 15 minutes, press START/PAUSE. Remove the basket and shake the potatoes for 10 seconds. Reinsert the basket and press START/PAUSE to resume cooking.
8. When cooking is complete, the frittata will pull away from the edges of the basket and the potatoes will be golden brown. Transfer the frittata to a cutting board and cut into 4 portions. Serve with the potatoes.

Nutrition:

- (Per serving) Calories: 307; Total fat: 17g; Saturated fat: 5.5g; Carbohydrates: 18g; Fiber: 1g; Protein: 19g; Sodium: 600mg

Sesame Bagels

Servings: 4

Cooking Time: 15 Minutes

Ingredients:

- 125g self-rising flour
- 240g non-fat plain Greek yoghurt
- 1 beaten egg
- 30g sesame seeds

Directions:

1. Combine the self-rising flour and Greek yoghurt in a medium mixing bowl using a wooden spoon.
2. Knead the dough for about 5 minutes on a lightly floured board.
3. Divide the dough into four equal pieces and roll each into a thin rope, securing the ends to form a bagel shape. Sprinkle the sesame seeds on it.
4. Press either "Zone 1" or "Zone 2" and then rotate the knob to select "Air Fryer".
5. Set the temperature to 140 degrees C, and then set the time for 3 minutes to preheat.
6. After preheating, arrange bagels into the basket.
7. Slide basket into Air Fryer and set the time for 15 minutes.
8. After cooking time is completed, remove both pans from Air Fryer.
9. Place the bagels onto a wire rack to cool for about 10 minutes and serve.

French Toasts

Servings: 4

Cooking Time: 6 Minutes

Ingredients:

- 4 eggs
- 120g evaporated milk
- 6 tablespoons sugar
- 4 teaspoons olive oil
- ¼ teaspoon ground cinnamon
- ¼ teaspoon vanilla extract
- 8 bread slices

Directions:

1. Line each basket of "Zone 1" and "Zone 2" with a greased piece of foil.
2. Then Press your chosen zone - "Zone 1" or "Zone 2" and then rotate the knob to select "Air Fry".
3. Set the temperature to 200 degrees C and then set the time for 5 minutes to preheat.
4. In a large bowl, add all ingredients except for bread slices and beat until well combined.
5. Coat the bread slices with egg mixture evenly.
6. After preheating, arrange 4 bread slices into the basket of each zone.
7. Slide the basket into the Air Fryer and set the time for 6 minutes.
8. While cooking, flip the slices once halfway through.
9. After cooking time is completed, remove the French toasts from Air Fryer and serve warm.

Jelly Doughnuts

Servings: 4

Cooking Time: 6 Minutes

Ingredients:

- 1 package Pillsbury Grands
- ½ cup seedless raspberry jelly
- 1 tablespoon butter, melted
- ½ cup sugar

Directions:

1. Spread the Pillsbury dough and cut out 3 inches round doughnuts out of it.
2. Place the doughnuts in the air fryer baskets and brush them with butter.
3. Drizzle sugar over the doughnuts.
4. Return the air fryer basket 1 to Zone 1, and basket 2 to Zone 2 of the Tefal 2-Basket Air Fryer.
5. Choose the "Air Fry" mode for Zone 1 at 320 degrees F and 6 minutes of cooking time.
6. Select the "MATCH COOK" option to copy the settings for Zone 2.
7. Initiate cooking by pressing the START/PAUSE BUTTON.
8. Use a piping bag to inject raspberry jelly into each doughnut.
9. Serve.

Nutrition:

- (Per serving) Calories 102 | Fat 7.6g |Sodium 545mg | Carbs 1.5g | Fiber 0.4g | Sugar 0.7g | Protein 7.1g

Baked Eggs

Servings: 10

Cooking Time: 12 Minutes

Ingredients:

- 450g marinara sauce, divided
- 2 tablespoons capers, drained and divided
- 16 eggs
- 120g whipping cream, divided
- 50g Parmesan cheese, shredded and divided
- Salt and ground black pepper, as required

Directions:

1. Press "Zone 1" and "Zone 2" and then rotate the knob to select "Bake".
2. Set the temperature to 200 degrees C and then set the time for 5 minutes to preheat.
3. Divide the marinara sauce in the bottom of 8 greased ramekins evenly and top with capers.
4. Carefully crack 2 eggs over marinara sauce into each ramekin and top with cream, followed by the Parmesan cheese.
5. Sprinkle each ramekin with salt and black pepper.
6. After preheating, arrange the ramekins into the basket of each zone.
7. Slide the basket into the Air Fryer and set the time for 12 minutes.
8. After cooking time is completed, remove the ramekins from Air Fryer.
9. Serve hot.

Breakfast Bacon

Servings: 4
Cooking Time: 14 Minutes.
Ingredients:

- ½ lb. bacon slices

Directions:

1. Spread half of the bacon slices in each of the crisper plate evenly in a single layer.
2. Return the crisper plate to the Tefal Dual Zone Air Fryer.
3. Choose the Air Fry mode for Zone 1 and set the temperature to 390 degrees F and the time to 14 minutes.
4. Select the "MATCH" button to copy the settings for Zone 2.
5. Initiate cooking by pressing the START/STOP button.
6. Flip the crispy bacon once cooked halfway through, then resume cooking.
7. Serve.

Nutrition:

- (Per serving) Calories 273 | Fat 22g |Sodium 517mg | Carbs 3.3g | Fiber 0.2g | Sugar 1.4g | Protein 16.1g

Breakfast Cheese Sandwich

Servings: 2
Cooking Time: 8 Minutes
Ingredients:

- 4 bread slices
- 2 provolone cheese slice
- ¼ tsp dried basil
- 2 tbsp mayonnaise
- 2 Monterey jack cheese slice
- 2 cheddar cheese slice
- ¼ tsp dried oregano

Directions:

1. In a small bowl, mix mayonnaise, basil, and oregano.
2. Spread mayonnaise on one side of the two bread slices.
3. Top two bread slices with cheddar cheese, provolone cheese, Monterey jack cheese slice, and cover with remaining bread slices.
4. Insert a crisper plate in the Tefal air fryer baskets.
5. Place sandwiches in both baskets.
6. Select zone 1, then select "air fry" mode and set the temperature to 390 degrees F for 8 minutes. Press "match" to match zone 2 settings to zone 1. Press "start/stop" to begin. Turn halfway through.

Nutrition:

- (Per serving) Calories 421 | Fat 30.7g |Sodium 796mg | Carbs 13.9g | Fiber 0.5g | Sugar 2.2g | Protein 22.5g

Vanilla Strawberry Doughnuts

Servings: 8
Cooking Time: 15 Minutes
Ingredients:

- 1 egg
- ½ cup strawberries, diced
- 80ml cup milk
- 1 tsp cinnamon
- 1 tsp baking soda
- 136g all-purpose flour
- 2 tsp vanilla
- 2 tbsp butter, melted
- 73g sugar
- ½ tsp salt

Directions:

1. In a bowl, mix flour, cinnamon, baking soda, sugar, and salt.
2. In a separate bowl, whisk egg, milk, butter, and vanilla.
3. Pour egg mixture into the flour mixture and mix until well combined.
4. Add strawberries and mix well.
5. Pour batter into the silicone doughnut moulds.
6. Insert a crisper plate in the Tefal air fryer baskets.
7. Place doughnut moulds in both baskets.
8. Select zone 1, then select "air fry" mode and set the temperature to 320 degrees F for 15 minutes. Press "match" to match zone 2 settings to zone 1. Press "start/stop" to begin.

Nutrition:

- (Per serving) Calories 133 | Fat 3.8g |Sodium 339mg | Carbs 21.9g | Fiber 0.8g | Sugar 9.5g | Protein 2.7g

Pumpkin French Toast Casserole With Sweet And Spicy Twisted Bacon

Servings:4
Cooking Time: 35 Minutes
Ingredients:

- FOR THE FRENCH TOAST CASSEROLE
- 3 large eggs
- 1 cup unsweetened almond milk
- 1 cup canned unsweetened pumpkin puree
- 2 teaspoons pumpkin pie spice
- ¼ cup packed light brown sugar
- 1 teaspoon vanilla extract
- 6 cups French bread cubes
- 1 teaspoon vegetable oil
- ¼ cup maple syrup
- FOR THE BACON
- 2 tablespoons light brown sugar
- ⅛ teaspoon cayenne pepper
- 8 slices bacon

Directions:

1. To prep the French toast casserole: In a shallow bowl, whisk together the eggs, almond milk, pumpkin puree, pumpkin pie spice, brown sugar, and vanilla.
2. Add the bread cubes to the egg mixture, making sure the bread is fully coated in the custard. Let sit for at least 10 minutes to allow the bread to soak up the custard.
3. To prep the bacon: In a small bowl, combine the brown sugar and cayenne.
4. Arrange the bacon on a cutting board in a single layer. Evenly sprinkle the strips with the brown sugar mixture. Fold the bacon strip in half lengthwise. Hold one end of the bacon steady and twist the other end so the bacon resembles a straw.
5. To cook the casserole and bacon: Brush the Zone 1 basket with the oil. Pour the French toast casserole into the Zone 1 basket, drizzle with maple syrup, and insert the basket in the unit. Install a crisper plate in the Zone 2 basket, add the bacon twists in a single layer, and insert the basket in the unit. For the best fit, arrange the bacon twists across the unit, front to back.
6. Select Zone 1, select BAKE, set the temperature to 330°F, and set the time to 35 minutes.
7. Select Zone 2, select AIR FRY, set the temperature to 400°F, and set the time to 12 minutes. Select SMART FINISH.
8. Press START/PAUSE to begin cooking.
9. When cooking is complete, transfer the bacon to a plate lined with paper towels. Let cool for 2 to 3 minutes before serving with the French toast casserole.

Nutrition:

- (Per serving) Calories: 601; Total fat: 28g; Saturated fat: 9g; Carbohydrates: 67g; Fiber: 2.5g; Protein: 17g; Sodium: 814mg

Blueberry Muffins

Servings: 12
Cooking Time: 12 Minutes
Ingredients:

- 2 egg, beaten
- 2 ripe bananas, peeled and mashed
- 220g almond flour
- 4 tablespoons granulated sugar
- 1 teaspoon baking powder
- 2 tablespoons coconut oil, melted
- 80g maple syrup
- 2 teaspoons apple cider vinegar
- 2 teaspoons vanilla extract
- 2 teaspoons lemon zest, grated
- Pinch of ground cinnamon
- 150g fresh blueberries

Directions:

1. In a large bowl, add all the ingredients except blueberries and mix until well combined.
2. Gently fold in the blueberries.
3. Grease 2 muffin tins.
4. Place the mixture into prepared muffin cups about ¾ full.
5. Press your chosen zone - "Zone 1" or "Zone 2" and then rotate the knob to select "Bake".
6. Set the temperature to 190 degrees C and then set the time for 5 minutes to preheat.
7. After preheating, arrange 1 muffin tin into the basket of each zone.
8. Slide the basket into the Air Fryer and set the time for 12 minutes.
9. After cooking time is completed, remove the muffin tins from Air Fryer.
10. Place both tins onto a wire rack to cool for 10 minutes.
11. Invert the blueberry muffins onto the wire rack to cool completely before serving.

Asparagus And Bell Pepper Strata And Greek Bagels

Servings: 6

Cooking Time: 14 To 20 Minutes

Ingredients:

- Asparagus and Bell Pepper Strata:
- 8 large asparagus spears, trimmed and cut into 2-inch pieces
- 80 ml shredded carrot
- 120 ml chopped red pepper
- 2 slices wholemeal bread, cut into ½-inch cubes
- 3 egg whites
- 1 egg
- 3 tablespoons 1% milk
- ½ teaspoon dried thyme
- Greek Bagels:
- 120 ml self-raising flour, plus more for dusting
- 120 ml plain Greek yoghurt
- 1 egg
- 1 tablespoon water
- 4 teaspoons sesame seeds or za'atar
- Cooking oil spray
- 1 tablespoon butter, melted

Directions:

1. Make the Asparagus and Bell Pepper Strata :
2. In a baking pan, combine the asparagus, carrot, red bell pepper, and 1 tablespoon of water. Bake in the air fryer at 166°C for 3 to 5 minutes, or until crisp-tender. Drain well.
3. Add the bread cubes to the vegetables and gently toss.
4. In a medium bowl, whisk the egg whites, egg, milk, and thyme until frothy.
5. Pour the egg mixture into the pan. Bake in the zone 1 drawer for 11 to 15 minutes, or until the strata is slightly puffy and set and the top starts to brown. Serve.
6. Make the Greek Bagels :
7. In a large bowl, using a wooden spoon, stir together the flour and yoghurt until a tacky dough forms. Transfer the dough to a lightly floured work surface and roll the dough into a ball.
8. Cut the dough into 2 pieces and roll each piece into a log. Form each log into a bagel shape, pinching the ends together.
9. In a small bowl, whisk the egg and water. Brush the egg wash on the bagels.
10. Sprinkle 2 teaspoons of the toppings on each bagel and gently press it into the dough.
11. Insert the crisper plate into the zone 2 drawer and the drawer into the unit. Preheat the drawer by selecting BAKE, setting the temperature to 166°C, and setting the time to 3 minutes. Select START/STOP to begin.
12. Once the drawer is preheated, spray the crisper plate with cooking spray. Drizzle the bagels with the butter and place them into the drawer.
13. Select BAKE, set the temperature to 166°C, and set the time to 10 minutes. Select START/STOP to begin.
14. When the cooking is complete, the bagels should be lightly golden on the outside. Serve warm.

Air Fried Bacon And Eggs

Servings: 1

Cooking Time: 10 Minutes

Ingredients:

- 2 eggs
- 2 slices bacon

Directions:

1. Grease a ramekin using cooking spray.
2. Install the crisper plate in the zone 1 drawer and place the bacon inside it. Insert the drawer into the unit.
3. Crack the eggs and add them to the greased ramekin.
4. Install the crisper plate in the zone 2 drawer and place the ramekin inside it. Insert the drawer into the unit.
5. Select zone 1 to AIR FRY for 9–11 minutes at 400 degrees F/ 200 degrees C. Select zone 2 to AIR FRY for 8–9 minutes at 350 degrees F/ 175 degrees C. Press SYNC.
6. Press START/STOP to begin cooking.
7. Enjoy!

Nutrition:

- (Per serving) Calories 331 | Fat 24.5g | Sodium 1001mg | Carbs 1.2g | Fiber 0g | Sugar 0.7g | Protein 25.3g

Cheesy Bell Pepper Eggs

Servings: 4
Cooking Time: 15 Minutes
Ingredients:

- 4 medium green peppers
- 85 g cooked ham, chopped
- ¼ medium onion, peeled and chopped
- 8 large eggs
- 235 ml mild Cheddar cheese

Directions:

1. Cut the tops off each pepper. Remove the seeds and the white membranes with a small knife. Place ham and onion into each pepper.
2. Crack 2 eggs into each pepper. Top with 60 ml cheese per pepper. Place into the zone 1 air fryer basket.
3. Adjust the temperature to 200°C and air fry for 15 minutes.
4. When fully cooked, peppers will be tender and eggs will be firm. Serve immediately.

Easy Sausage Pizza

Servings: 4
Cooking Time: 6 Minutes
Ingredients:

- 2 tablespoons ketchup
- 1 pitta bread
- 80 ml sausage meat
- 230 g Mozzarella cheese
- 1 teaspoon garlic powder
- 1 tablespoon olive oil

Directions:

1. Preheat the air fryer to 170°C.
2. Spread the ketchup over the pitta bread.
3. Top with the sausage meat and cheese. Sprinkle with the garlic powder and olive oil.
4. Put the pizza in the zone 1 air fryer basket and bake for 6 minutes.
5. Serve warm.

Egg And Bacon Muffins

Servings: 1
Cooking Time: 15 Minutes
Ingredients:

- 2 eggs
- Salt and ground black pepper, to taste
- 1 tablespoon green pesto
- 85 g shredded Cheddar cheese
- 140 g cooked bacon
- 1 spring onion, chopped

Directions:

1. Line a cupcake tin with parchment paper. Beat the eggs with pepper, salt, and pesto in a bowl. Mix in the cheese.
2. Pour the eggs into the cupcake tin and top with the bacon and spring onion.
3. Place the cupcake tin into the zone 1 drawer and bake at 180°C for 15 minutes, or until the egg is set. Serve immediately.

Sweet Potato Hash

Servings: 4
Cooking Time: 15 Minutes
Ingredients:

- 3 sweet potatoes, peel & cut into ½-inch pieces
- ½ tsp cinnamon
- 2 tbsp olive oil
- 1 bell pepper, cut into ½-inch pieces
- ½ tsp dried thyme
- ½ tsp nutmeg
- 1 medium onion, cut into ½-inch pieces
- Pepper
- Salt

Directions:

1. In a bowl, toss sweet potatoes with the remaining ingredients.
2. Insert a crisper plate in Tefal air fryer baskets.
3. Add potato mixture in both baskets.
4. Select zone 1 then select "air fry" mode and set the temperature to 355 degrees F for 15 minutes. Press "match" to match zone 2 settings to zone 1. Press "start/stop" to begin.

Nutrition:

- (Per serving) Calories 167 | Fat 7.3g |Sodium 94mg | Carbs 24.9g | Fiber 4.2g | Sugar 6.8g | Protein 2.2g

Breakfast Meatballs

Servings: 18 Meatballs
Cooking Time: 15 Minutes
Ingredients:

- 450 g pork sausage meat, removed from casings
- ½ teaspoon salt
- ¼ teaspoon ground black pepper
- 120 ml shredded sharp Cheddar cheese
- 30 g cream cheese, softened
- 1 large egg, whisked

Directions:

1. Combine all ingredients in a large bowl. Form mixture into eighteen 1-inch meatballs.
2. Place meatballs into the two ungreased air fryer drawers. Adjust the temperature to 204°C and air fry for 15 minutes, shaking drawers three times during cooking. Meatballs will be browned on the outside and have an internal temperature of at least 64°C when completely cooked. Serve warm.

Breakfast Stuffed Peppers

Servings: 4
Cooking Time: 13 Minutes
Ingredients:

- 2 capsicums, halved, seeds removed
- 4 eggs
- 1 teaspoon olive oil
- 1 pinch salt and pepper
- 1 pinch sriracha flakes

Directions:

1. Cut each capsicum in half and place two halves in each air fryer basket.
2. Crack one egg into each capsicum and top it with black pepper, salt, sriracha flakes and olive oil.
3. Return the air fryer basket 1 to Zone 1, and basket 2 to Zone 2 of the Tefal 2-Basket Air Fryer.
4. Choose the "Air Fry" mode for Zone 1 at 390 degrees F and 13 minutes of cooking time.
5. Select the "MATCH COOK" option to copy the settings for Zone 2.
6. Initiate cooking by pressing the START/PAUSE BUTTON.
7. Serve warm.

Nutrition:

- (Per serving) Calories 237 | Fat 19g |Sodium 518mg | Carbs 7g | Fiber 1.5g | Sugar 3.4g | Protein 12g

Onion Omelette And Buffalo Egg Cups

Servings: 4
Cooking Time: 15 Minutes
Ingredients:

- Onion Omelette:
- 3 eggs
- Salt and ground black pepper, to taste
- ½ teaspoons soy sauce
- 1 large onion, chopped
- 2 tablespoons grated Cheddar cheese
- Cooking spray
- Buffalo Egg Cups:
- 4 large eggs
- 60 g full-fat cream cheese
- 2 tablespoons buffalo sauce
- 120 ml shredded sharp Cheddar cheese

Directions:

1. Make the Onion Omelette :
2. Preheat the zone 1 air fryer drawer to 180°C.
3. In a bowl, whisk together the eggs, salt, pepper, and soy sauce.
4. Spritz a small pan with cooking spray. Spread the chopped onion across the bottom of the pan, then transfer the pan to the zone 1 air fryer drawer.
5. Bake in the preheated air fryer for 6 minutes or until the onion is translucent.
6. Add the egg mixture on top of the onions to coat well. Add the cheese on top, then continue baking for another 6 minutes.
7. Allow to cool before serving.
8. Make the Buffalo Egg Cups :
9. Crack eggs into two ramekins.
10. In a small microwave-safe bowl, mix cream cheese, buffalo sauce, and Cheddar. Microwave for 20 seconds and then stir. Place a spoonful into each ramekin on top of the eggs.
11. Place ramekins into the zone 2 air fryer drawer.
12. Adjust the temperature to 160°C and bake for 15 minutes.
13. Serve warm.

Glazed Apple Fritters Glazed Peach Fritters

Servings:4
Cooking Time: 12 Minutes
Ingredients:

- FOR THE FRITTERS
- ¾ cup all-purpose flour
- 2 tablespoons granulated sugar
- 1 teaspoon baking powder
- ½ teaspoon kosher salt
- ½ teaspoon ground cinnamon
- ⅓ cup whole milk
- 2 tablespoons cold unsalted butter, grated
- 1 large egg
- 1 teaspoon fresh lemon juice
- 1 apple, peeled and diced
- 1 peach, peeled and diced
- FOR THE GLAZE
- ½ cup powdered sugar
- 1 tablespoon whole milk
- ½ teaspoon vanilla extract
- ½ teaspoon ground cinnamon
- Pinch salt

Directions:

1. To prep the fritters: In a large bowl, combine the flour, granulated sugar, baking powder, salt, and cinnamon. Stir in the milk, butter, egg, and lemon juice to form a thick batter.
2. Transfer half of the batter to a second bowl. Fold the apples into one bowl and the peaches into the other.
3. To prep the glaze: In a small bowl, whisk together the powdered sugar, milk, vanilla, cinnamon, and salt until smooth. Set aside.
4. To cook the fritters: Install a crisper plate in each of the two baskets. Drop two ¼-cup scoops of the apple fritter batter into the Zone 1 basket and insert the basket in the unit. Drop two ¼-cup scoops of the peach fritter batter into the Zone 2 basket and insert the basket in the unit.
5. Select Zone 1, select AIR FRY, set the temperature to 345°F, and set the time to 10 minutes.
6. Select Zone 2, select AIR FRY, set the temperature to 345°F, and set the time to 12 minutes. Select SMART FINISH.
7. Press START/PAUSE to begin cooking.
8. When cooking is complete, transfer the fritters to a wire rack and drizzle the glaze over them. Serve warm or at room temperature.

Nutrition:

- (Per serving) Calories: 298; Total fat: 8g; Saturated fat: 4.5g; Carbohydrates: 53g; Fiber: 3g; Protein: 5g; Sodium: 170mg

Quick And Easy Blueberry Muffins

Servings: 8 Muffins
Cooking Time: 12 Minutes
Ingredients:

- 315 ml flour
- 120 ml sugar
- 2 teaspoons baking powder
- ¼ teaspoon salt
- 80 ml rapeseed oil
- 1 egg
- 120 ml milk
- 160 ml blueberries, fresh or frozen and thawed

Directions:

1. Preheat the air fryer to 165°C.
2. In a medium bowl, stir together flour, sugar, baking powder, and salt.
3. In a separate bowl, combine oil, egg, and milk and mix well.
4. Add egg mixture to dry ingredients and stir just until moistened.
5. Gently stir in the blueberries.
6. Spoon batter evenly into parchment paper-lined muffin cups.
7. Put the muffin cups in the two air fryer baskets and bake for 12 minutes or until tops spring back when touched lightly.
8. Serve immediately.

Fish And Seafood Recipes

Fried Prawns

Servings: 4
Cooking Time: 5 Minutes
Ingredients:

- 70 g self-raising flour
- 1 teaspoon paprika
- 1 teaspoon salt
- ½ teaspoon freshly ground black pepper
- 1 large egg, beaten
- 120 g finely crushed panko bread crumbs
- 20 frozen large prawns (about 900 g), peeled and deveined
- Cooking spray

Directions:

1. In a shallow bowl, whisk the flour, paprika, salt, and pepper until blended. Add the beaten egg to a second shallow bowl and the bread crumbs to a third.
2. One at a time, dip the prawns into the flour, the egg, and the bread crumbs, coating thoroughly.
3. Preheat the air fryer to 205°C. Line the two air fryer baskets with baking paper.
4. Place the prawns on the baking paper and spritz with oil.
5. Air fry for 2 minutes. Shake the baskets, spritz the prawns with oil, and air fry for 3 minutes more until lightly browned and crispy. Serve hot.

Two-way Salmon

Servings:2
Cooking Time:18
Ingredients:

- 2 salmon fillets, 8 ounces each
- 2 tablespoons of Cajun seasoning
- 2 tablespoons of jerk seasoning
- 1 lemon cut in half
- oil spray, for greasing

Directions:

1. First, drizzle lemon juice over the salmon and wash it with tap water.
2. Rinse and pat dry the fillets with a paper towel.
3. Now rub o fillet with Cajun seasoning and grease it with oil spray.
4. Take the second fillet and rub it with jerk seasoning.
5. Grease the second fillet of salmon with oil spray.
6. now put the salmon fillets in both the baskets.
7. Set the Zone 1 basket to 390 degrees F for 16-18 minutes
8. Select MATCH button for zone 2 basket.
9. hit the start button to start cooking.
10. Once the cooking is done, serve the fish hot with mayonnaise.

Nutrition:

- (Per serving) Calories 238| Fat 11.8g| Sodium 488mg | Carbs 9g | Fiber 0g | Sugar8 g | Protein 35g

Crusted Tilapia

Servings: 4
Cooking Time: 17 Minutes
Ingredients:

- ¾ cup breadcrumbs
- 1 packet dry ranch-style dressing
- 2 ½ tablespoons vegetable oil
- 2 eggs beaten
- 4 tilapia fillets
- Herbs and chilies to garnish

Directions:

1. Thoroughly mix ranch dressing with panko in a bowl.
2. Whisk eggs in a shallow bowl.
3. Dip each fish fillet in the egg, then coat evenly with the panko mixture.
4. Set two coated fillets in each of the crisper plate.
5. Return the crisper plates to the Tefal Dual Zone Air Fryer.
6. Choose the Air Fry mode for Zone 1 and set the temperature to 390 degrees F and the time to 17 minutes|
7. Select the "MATCH" button to copy the settings for Zone 2.
8. Initiate cooking by pressing the START/STOP button.
9. Serve warm with herbs and chilies.

Frozen Breaded Fish Fillet

Servings:2

Cooking Time:12

Ingredients:

- 4 Frozen Breaded Fish Fillet
- Oil spray, for greasing
- 1 cup mayonnaise

Directions:

1. Take the frozen fish fillets out of the bag and place them in both baskets of the air fryer.
2. Lightly grease it with oil spray.
3. Set the Zone 1 basket to 380 degrees F fo12 minutes.
4. Select the MATCH button for the zone 2 basket.
5. hit the start button to start cooking.
6. Once the cooking is done, serve the fish hot with mayonnaise.

Nutrition:

- (Per serving) Calories 921| Fat 61.5g| Sodium 1575mg | Carbs 69g | Fiber 2g | Sugar 9.5g | Protein 29.1g

Fish Tacos

Servings: 5

Cooking Time: 30 Minutes

Ingredients:

- 1 pound firm white fish such as cod, haddock, pollock, halibut, or walleye
- ¾ cup gluten-free flour blend
- 3 eggs
- 1 cup gluten-free panko breadcrumbs
- 1 teaspoon garlic powder
- 1 teaspoon onion powder
- 1 teaspoon cumin
- 1 teaspoon lemon pepper
- 1 teaspoon red chili flakes
- 1 teaspoon kosher salt, divided
- 1 teaspoon pepper, divided
- Cooking oil spray
- 1 package corn tortillas
- Toppings such as tomatoes, avocado, cabbage, radishes, jalapenos, salsa, or hot sauce (optional)

Directions:

1. Dry the fish with paper towels. (Make sure to thaw the fish if it's frozen.) Depending on the size of the fillets, cut the fish in half or thirds.
2. On both sides of the fish pieces, liberally season with salt and pepper.
3. Put the flour in a dish.
4. In a separate bowl, crack the eggs and whisk them together until well blended.
5. Put the panko breadcrumbs in another bowl. Add the garlic powder, onion powder, cumin, lemon pepper, and red chili flakes. Add salt and pepper to taste. Stir until everything is well blended.
6. Each piece of fish should be dipped in the flour, then the eggs, and finally in the breadcrumb mixture. Make sure that each piece is completely coated.
7. Put a crisper plate in each drawer. Arrange the fish pieces in a single layer in each drawer. Insert the drawers into the unit.
8. Select zone 1, then AIR FRY, then set the temperature to 360 degrees F/ 180 degrees C with a 20-minute timer. To match zone 2 settings to zone 1, choose MATCH. To begin, select START/STOP.
9. Remove the fish from the drawers after the timer has finished. Place the crispy fish on warmed tortillas.

Nutrition:

- (Per serving) Calories 534 | Fat 18g | Sodium 679mg | Carbs 63g | Fiber 8g | Sugar 3g | Protein 27g

Coconut Cream Mackerel

Servings: 4

Cooking Time: 6 Minutes

Ingredients:

- 900 g mackerel fillet
- 240 ml coconut cream
- 1 teaspoon ground coriander
- 1 teaspoon cumin seeds
- 1 garlic clove, peeled, chopped

Directions:

1. Chop the mackerel roughly and sprinkle it with coconut cream, ground coriander, cumin seeds, and garlic.
2. Then put the fish in the two air fryer drawers and cook at 204°C for 6 minutes.

Broiled Teriyaki Salmon With Eggplant In Stir-fry Sauce

Servings:4
Cooking Time: 25 Minutes
Ingredients:

- FOR THE TERIYAKI SALMON
- 4 salmon fillets (6 ounces each)
- ½ cup teriyaki sauce
- 3 scallions, sliced
- FOR THE EGGPLANT
- ¼ cup reduced-sodium soy sauce
- ¼ cup packed light brown sugar
- 1 tablespoon minced fresh ginger
- 1 tablespoon minced garlic
- 2 teaspoons sesame oil
- ¼ teaspoon red pepper flakes
- 1 eggplant, peeled and cut into bite-size cubes
- Nonstick cooking spray

Directions:

1. To prep the teriyaki salmon: Brush the top of each salmon fillet with the teriyaki sauce.
2. To prep the eggplant: In a small bowl, whisk together the soy sauce, brown sugar, ginger, garlic, sesame oil, and red pepper flakes. Set the stir-fry sauce aside.
3. Spritz the eggplant cubes with cooking spray.
4. To cook the salmon and eggplant: Install a crisper plate in each of the two baskets. Place the salmon in a single layer in the Zone 1 basket and insert the basket in the unit. Place the eggplant in the Zone 2 basket and insert the basket in the unit.
5. Select Zone 1, select AIR BROIL, set the temperature to 450°F, and set the time to 8 minutes.
6. Select Zone 2, select AIR FRY, set the temperature to 390°F, and set the time to 25 minutes. Select SMART FINISH.
7. Press START/PAUSE to begin cooking.
8. When the Zone 2 timer reads 5 minutes, press START/PAUSE. Remove the basket and pour the stir-fry sauce evenly over the eggplant. Shake or stir to coat the eggplant cubes in the sauce. Reinsert the basket and press START/PAUSE to resume cooking.
9. When cooking is complete, the salmon should be cooked to your liking and the eggplant tender and slightly caramelized. Serve hot.

Nutrition:

- (Per serving) Calories: 499; Total fat: 22g; Saturated fat: 2g; Carbohydrates: 36g; Fiber: 3.5g; Protein: 42g; Sodium: 1,024mg

Stuffed Mushrooms With Crab

Servings: 4
Cooking Time: 18 Minutes
Ingredients:

- 907g baby bella mushrooms
- cooking spray
- 2 teaspoons tony chachere's salt blend
- ¼ red onion, diced
- 2 celery ribs, diced
- 227g lump crab
- ½ cup seasoned bread crumbs
- 1 large egg
- ½ cup parmesan cheese, shredded
- 1 teaspoon oregano
- 1 teaspoon hot sauce

Directions:

1. Mix all the ingredients except the mushrooms in a bowl.
2. Divide the crab filling into the mushroom caps.
3. Place the caps in the air fryer baskets.
4. Return the air fryer basket 1 to Zone 1, and basket 2 to Zone 2 of the Tefal 2-Basket Air Fryer.
5. Choose the "Air Fry" mode for Zone 1 at 400 degrees F and 18 minutes of cooking time.
6. Select the "MATCH COOK" option to copy the settings for Zone 2.
7. Initiate cooking by pressing the START/PAUSE BUTTON.
8. Serve warm.

Nutrition:

- (Per serving) Calories 399 | Fat 16g |Sodium 537mg | Carbs 28g | Fiber 3g | Sugar 10g | Protein 35g

Italian Baked Cod

Servings: 4
Cooking Time: 12 Minutes

Ingredients:

- 4 cod fillets, 170 g each
- 2 tablespoons salted butter, melted
- 1 teaspoon Italian seasoning
- ¼ teaspoon salt
- 120 ml tomato-based pasta sauce

Directions:

1. Place cod into an ungreased round nonstick baking dish. Pour butter over cod and sprinkle with Italian seasoning and salt. Top with pasta sauce.
2. Place dish into the two air fryer drawers. Adjust the temperature to 176°C and bake for 12 minutes. Fillets will be lightly browned, easily flake, and have an internal temperature of at least 64°C when done. Serve warm.

Chilean Sea Bass With Olive Relish And Snapper With Tomato

Servings: 4
Cooking Time: 15 Minutes

Ingredients:

- Chilean Sea Bass with Olive Relish:
- Olive oil spray
- 2 (170 g) Chilean sea bass fillets or other firm-fleshed white fish
- 3 tablespoons extra-virgin olive oil
- ½ teaspoon ground cumin
- ½ teaspoon kosher or coarse sea salt
- ½ teaspoon black pepper
- 60 g pitted green olives, diced
- 10 g finely diced onion
- 1 teaspoon chopped capers
- Snapper with Tomato:
- 2 snapper fillets
- 1 shallot, peeled and sliced
- 2 garlic cloves, halved
- 1 bell pepper, sliced
- 1 small-sized serrano pepper, sliced
- 1 tomato, sliced
- 1 tablespoon olive oil
- ¼ teaspoon freshly ground black pepper
- ½ teaspoon paprika
- Sea salt, to taste
- 2 bay leaves

Directions:

1. Make the Chilean Sea Bass with Olive Relish :
2. Spray the zone 1 air fryer drawer with the olive oil spray. Drizzle the fillets with the olive oil and sprinkle with the cumin, salt, and pepper. Place the fish in the zone 1 air fryer drawer. Set the air fryer to 164°C for 10 minutes, or until the fish flakes easily with a fork.
3. Meanwhile, in a small bowl, stir together the olives, onion, and capers.
4. Serve the fish topped with the relish.
5. Make the Snapper with Tomato :
6. Place two baking paper sheets on a working surface. Place the fish in the center of one side of the baking paper.
7. Top with the shallot, garlic, peppers, and tomato. Drizzle olive oil over the fish and vegetables. Season with black pepper, paprika, and salt. Add the bay leaves.
8. Fold over the other half of the baking paper. Now, fold the paper around the edges tightly and create a half moon shape, sealing the fish inside.
9. Cook in the zone 2 air fryer drawer at 200°C for 15 minutes. Serve warm.

Seasoned Tuna Steaks

Servings: 4
Cooking Time: 9 Minutes

Ingredients:

- 1 teaspoon garlic powder
- ½ teaspoon salt
- ¼ teaspoon dried thyme
- ¼ teaspoon dried oregano
- 4 tuna steaks
- 2 tablespoons olive oil
- 1 lemon, quartered

Directions:

1. Preheat the air fryer to 190°C.
2. In a small bowl, whisk together the garlic powder, salt, thyme, and oregano.
3. Coat the tuna steaks with olive oil. Season both sides of each steak with the seasoning blend. Place the steaks in a single layer in the two air fryer baskets.
4. Roast for 5 minutes, then flip and roast for an additional 3 to 4 minutes.

Salmon With Broccoli And Cheese

Servings:2
Cooking Time:18

Ingredients:

- 2 cups of broccoli
- ½ cup of butter, melted
- Salt and pepper, to taste
- Oil spray, for greasing
- 1 cup of grated cheddar cheese
- 1 pound of salmon, fillets

Directions:

1. Take a bowl and add broccoli to it.
2. Add salt and black pepper and spray it with oil.
3. Put the broccoli in the air fryer zone 1 backset.
4. Now rub the salmon fillets with salt, black pepper, and butter.
5. Put it into zone 2 baskets.
6. Set zone 1 to air fry mode for 5 minters at 400 degrees F.
7. Set zone 2 to air fry mode for 18 minutes at 390 degrees F.
8. Hit start to start the cooking.
9. Once done, serve and by placing it on serving plates.
10. Put the grated cheese on top of the salmon and serve.

Nutrition:

- (Per serving) Calories 966 | Fat 79.1 g| Sodium 808 mg | Carbs 6.8 g | Fiber 2.4g | Sugar 1.9g | Protein 61.2 g

Crusted Cod

Servings: 4
Cooking Time: 13 Minutes

Ingredients:

- 2 lbs. cod fillets
- Salt, to taste
- Freshly black pepper, to taste
- ½ cup all-purpose flour
- 1 large egg, beaten
- 2 cups panko bread crumbs
- 1 teaspoon Old Bay seasoning
- Lemon wedges, for serving
- Tartar sauce, for serving

Directions:

1. Rub the fish with salt and black pepper.
2. Add flour in one shallow bowl, beat eggs in another bowl, and mix panko with Old Bay in a shallow bowl.
3. First coat the fish with flour, then dip it in the eggs and finally coat it with the panko mixture.
4. Place half of the seasoned codfish in each crisper plate.
5. Return the crisper plates to the Tefal Dual Zone Air Fryer.
6. Choose the Air Fry mode for Zone 1 and set the temperature to 390 degrees F and the time to 13 minutes|
7. Select the "MATCH" button to copy the settings for Zone 2.
8. Initiate cooking by pressing the START/STOP button.
9. Flip the fish once cooked halfway, then resume cooking.
10. Serve warm and fresh with tartar sauce and lemon wedges.

Honey Sriracha Mahi Mahi

Servings: 4
Cooking Time: 7 Minutes

Ingredients:

- 3 pounds mahi-mahi
- 6 tablespoons honey
- 4 tablespoons sriracha
- Salt, to taste
- Cooking spray

Directions:

1. In a small bowl, mix the sriracha sauce and honey. Mix well.
2. Season the fish with salt and pour the honey mixture over it. Let it sit at room temperature for 20 minutes.
3. Place a crisper plate in each drawer. Put the fish in a single layer in each. Insert the drawers into the unit.
4. Select zone 1, then AIR FRY, then set the temperature to 400 degrees F/ 200 degrees C with a 7-minute timer. To match zone 2 settings to zone 1, choose MATCH. To begin, select START/STOP.
5. Remove the fish from the drawers after the timer has finished.

Nutrition:

- (Per serving) Calories 581 | Fat 22g | Sodium 495mg | Carbs 26g | Fiber 4g | Sugar 26g | Protein 68g

Codfish With Herb Vinaigrette

Servings:2
Cooking Time:16
Ingredients:

- Vinaigrette Ingredients:
- 1/2 cup parsley leaves
- 1 cup basil leaves
- ½ cup mint leaves
- 2 tablespoons thyme leaves
- 1/4 teaspoon red pepper flakes
- 2 cloves of garlic
- 4 tablespoons of red wine vinegar
- ¼ cup of olive oil
- Salt, to taste
- Other Ingredients:
- 1.5 pounds fish fillets, cod fish
- 2 tablespoons olive oil
- Salt and black pepper, to taste
- 1 teaspoon of paprika
- 1teasbpoon of Italian seasoning

Directions:

1. Blend the entire vinaigrette ingredient in a high-speed blender and pulse into a smooth paste.
2. Set aside for drizzling overcooked fish.
3. Rub the fillets with salt, black pepper, paprika, Italian seasoning, and olive oil.
4. Divide it between two baskets of the air fryer.
5. Set the zone 1 to 16 minutes at 390 degrees F, at AIR FRY mode.
6. Press the MATCH button for the second basket.
7. Once done, serve the fillets with the drizzle of blended vinaigrette

Nutrition:

- (Per serving) Calories 1219| Fat 81.8g| Sodium 1906mg | Carbs64.4 g | Fiber5.5 g | Sugar 0.4g | Protein 52.1g

Healthy Lobster Cakes

Servings: 6
Cooking Time: 12 Minutes
Ingredients:

- 1 egg
- 145g cooked lobster meat
- 60g butter, melted
- 1 tbsp Cajun seasoning
- 50g breadcrumbs
- Pepper
- Salt

Directions:

1. In a shallow dish, add breadcrumbs, pepper, and salt.
2. In a bowl, mix lobster meat, Cajun seasoning, egg, and butter until well combined.
3. Make patties from the lobster meat mixture and coat with breadcrumbs.
4. Insert a crisper plate in the Tefal air fryer baskets.
5. Place the coated patties in both baskets.
6. Select zone 1, then select "bake" mode and set the temperature to 390 degrees F for 12 minutes. Press "match" to match zone 2 settings to zone 1. Press "start/stop" to begin.

Nutrition:

- (Per serving) Calories 119 | Fat 7.2g |Sodium 287mg | Carbs 6.6g | Fiber 0.4g | Sugar 0.6g | Protein 6.8g

Keto Baked Salmon With Pesto

Servings:2
Cooking Time:18
Ingredients:

- 4 salmon fillets, 2 inches thick
- 2 ounces green pesto
- Salt and black pepper
- ½ tablespoon of canola oil, for greasing
- 1-1/2 cup mayonnaise
- 2 tablespoons Greek yogurt
- Salt and black pepper, to taste

Directions:

1. Rub the salmon with pesto, salt, oil, and black pepper.
2. In a small bowl, whisk together all the green sauce ingredients.
3. Divide the fish fillets between both the baskets.
4. Set zone 1 to air fry mode for 18 minutes at 390 degrees F.
5. Select MATCH button for Zone 2 basket.
6. Once the cooking is done, serve it with green sauce drizzle.
7. Enjoy.

Nutrition:

- (Per serving) Calories 1165 | Fat80.7 g| Sodium 1087 mg | Carbs 33.1g | Fiber 0.5g | Sugar11.5 g | Protein 80.6g

Panko-crusted Fish Sticks

Servings: 4

Cooking Time: 15 Minutes

Ingredients:

- Tartar Sauce:
- 470 ml mayonnaise
- 2 tablespoons dill pickle relish
- 1 tablespoon dried minced onions
- Fish Sticks:
- Olive or vegetable oil, for spraying
- 455 g tilapia fillets
- 75 g plain flour
- 120 g panko bread crumbs
- 2 tablespoons Creole seasoning
- 2 teaspoons garlic granules
- 1 teaspoon onion powder
- ½ teaspoon salt
- ¼ teaspoon freshly ground black pepper
- 1 large egg

Directions:

1. Make the Tartar Sauce: In a small bowl, whisk together the mayonnaise, pickle relish, and onions. Cover with plastic wrap and refrigerate until ready to serve. You can make this sauce ahead of time; the flavors will intensify as it chills. Make the Fish Sticks: 2. Preheat the air fryer to 175°C. Line the two air fryer baskets with baking paper and spray lightly with oil. 3. Cut the fillets into equal-size sticks and place them in a zip-top plastic bag. 4. Add the flour to the bag, seal, and shake well until evenly coated. 5. In a shallow bowl, mix together the bread crumbs, Creole seasoning, garlic, onion powder, salt, and black pepper. 6. In a small bowl, whisk the egg. 7. Dip the fish sticks in the egg, then dredge in the bread crumb mixture until completely coated. 8. Place the fish sticks in the two prepared baskets. Do not overcrowd. Spray lightly with oil. 9. Cook for 12 to 15 minutes, or until browned and cooked through. Serve with the tartar sauce.

Brown Sugar Garlic Salmon

Servings: 4

Cooking Time: 10 Minutes

Ingredients:

- 455g salmon
- Salt and black pepper, to taste
- 2 tablespoons brown sugar
- 1 teaspoon chili powder
- ½ teaspoon paprika
- 1 teaspoon Italian seasoning
- 1 teaspoon garlic powder

Directions:

1. Mix brown sugar with garlic powder, Italian seasoning, paprika, and chili powder in a bowl.
2. Rub this mixture over the salmon along with black pepper and salt.
3. Place the salmon in the air fryer baskets.
4. Return the air fryer basket 1 to Zone 1, and basket 2 to Zone 2 of the Tefal 2-Basket Air Fryer.
5. Choose the "Air Fry" mode for Zone 1 and set the temperature to 400 degrees F and 10 minutes of cooking time.
6. Select the "MATCH COOK" option to copy the settings for Zone 2.
7. Initiate cooking by pressing the START/PAUSE BUTTON.
8. Flip the salmon once cooked halfway through.
9. Serve warm.

Nutrition:

- (Per serving) Calories 275 | Fat 1.4g |Sodium 582mg | Carbs 31.5g | Fiber 1.1g | Sugar 0.1g | Protein 29.8g

Bacon Halibut Steak

Servings: 4

Cooking Time: 10 Minutes

Ingredients:

- 680 g halibut steaks (170 g each fillet)
- 1 teaspoon avocado oil
- 1 teaspoon ground black pepper
- 110 g bacon, sliced

Directions:

1. Sprinkle the halibut steaks with avocado oil and ground black pepper.
2. Then wrap the fish in the bacon slices and put in the two air fryer baskets.
3. Cook the fish at 200°C for 5 minutes per side.

Flavorful Salmon With Green Beans

Servings: 4
Cooking Time: 10 Minutes

Ingredients:

- 4 ounces green beans
- 1 tablespoon canola oil
- 4 (6-ounce) salmon fillets
- 1⁄3 cup prepared sesame-ginger sauce
- Kosher salt, to taste
- Black pepper, to taste

Directions:

1. Toss the green beans with a teaspoon each of salt and pepper in a large bowl.
2. Place a crisper plate in each drawer. Place the green beans in the zone 1 drawer and insert it into the unit. Place the salmon into the zone 2 drawer and place it into the unit.
3. Select zone 1, then AIR FRY, and set the temperature to 390 degrees F/ 200 degrees C with a 10-minute timer.
4. Select zone 2, then AIR FRY, and set the temperature to 390 degrees F/ 200 degrees C with a 15-minute timer. Select SYNC. To begin cooking, press the START/STOP button.
5. Press START/STOP to pause the unit when the zone 2 timer reaches 9 minutes. Remove the salmon from the drawer and toss it in the sesame-ginger sauce. To resume cooking, replace the drawer in the device and press START/STOP.
6. When cooking is complete, serve the salmon and green beans immediately.

Nutrition:

- (Per serving) Calories 305 | Fat 16g | Sodium 535mg | Carbs 8.7g | Fiber 1g | Sugar 6.4g | Protein 34.9g

Crusted Shrimp

Servings: 4
Cooking Time: 13 Minutes

Ingredients:

- 1 lb. shrimp
- ½ cup flour, all-purpose
- 1 teaspoon salt
- ½ teaspoon baking powder
- ⅔ cup water
- 2 cups coconut shred
- ½ cup bread crumbs

Directions:

1. In a small bowl, whisk together flour, salt, water, and baking powder. Set aside for 5 minutes|
2. In another shallow bowl, toss bread crumbs with coconut shreds together.
3. Dredge shrimp in liquid, then coat in coconut mixture, making sure it's totally covered.
4. Repeat until all shrimp are coated.
5. Spread half of the shrimp in each crisper plate and spray them with cooking oil.
6. Return the crisper plates to the Tefal Dual Zone Air Fryer.
7. Choose the Air Fry mode for Zone 1 and set the temperature to 390 degrees F and the time to 13 minutes|
8. Select the "MATCH" button to copy the settings for Zone 2.
9. Initiate cooking by pressing the START/STOP button.
10. Shake the baskets once cooked halfway, then resume cooking.
11. Serve with your favorite dip.

Country Prawns

Servings: 4
Cooking Time: 15 To 20 Minutes

Ingredients:

- 455 g large prawns, peeled and deveined, with tails on
- 455 g smoked sausage, cut into thick slices
- 2 corn cobs, quartered
- 1 courgette, cut into bite-sized pieces
- 1 red bell pepper, cut into chunks
- 1 tablespoon Old Bay seasoning
- 2 tablespoons olive oil
- Cooking spray

Directions:

1. Preheat the air fryer to 204°C. Spray the air fryer drawer lightly with cooking spray.
2. In a large bowl, mix the prawns, sausage, corn, courgette, bell pepper, and Old Bay seasoning, and toss to coat with the spices. Add the olive oil and toss again until evenly coated.
3. Spread the mixture in the two air fryer drawers in a single layer.
4. Air fry for 15 to 20 minutes, or until cooked through, shaking the drawers every 5 minutes for even cooking.
5. Serve immediately.

"fried" Fish With Seasoned Potato Wedges

Servings:4
Cooking Time: 30 Minutes
Ingredients:

- FOR THE FISH
- 4 cod fillets (6 ounces each)
- 4 tablespoons all-purpose flour, divided
- 1/4 cup cornstarch
- 1 teaspoon baking powder
- 1/4 teaspoon kosher salt
- 1/3 cup lager-style beer or sparkling water
- Tartar sauce, cocktail sauce, or malt vinegar, for serving (optional)
- FOR THE POTATOES
- 4 russet potatoes
- 2 tablespoons vegetable oil
- 1/2 teaspoon paprika
- 1/2 teaspoon kosher salt
- 1/4 teaspoon garlic powder
- 1/4 teaspoon freshly ground black pepper

Directions:

1. To prep the fish: Pat the fish dry with a paper towel and coat lightly with 2 tablespoons of flour.
2. In a shallow dish, combine the remaining 2 tablespoons of flour, the cornstarch, baking powder, and salt. Stir in the beer to form a thick batter.
3. Dip the fish in the batter to coat both sides, then let rest on a cutting board for 10 minutes.
4. To prep the potatoes: Cut each potato in half lengthwise, then cut each half into 4 wedges.
5. In a large bowl, combine the potatoes and oil. Toss well to fully coat the potatoes. Add the paprika, salt, garlic powder, and black pepper and toss well to coat.
6. To cook the fish and potato wedges: Install a crisper plate in each of the two baskets. Place a piece of parchment paper or aluminum foil over the plate in the Zone 1 basket. Place the fish in the basket and insert the basket in the unit. Place the potato wedges in a single layer in the Zone 2 basket and insert the basket in the unit.
7. Select Zone 1, select AIR FRY, set the temperature to 400°F, and set the timer to 13 minutes.
8. Select Zone 2, select AIR FRY, set the temperature to 400°F, and set the timer to 30 minutes. Select SMART FINISH.
9. Press START/PAUSE to begin cooking.
10. When the Zone 1 timer reads 5 minutes, press START/PAUSE. Remove the basket and use a silicone spatula to carefully flip the fish over. Reinsert the basket and press START/PAUSE to resume cooking.
11. When cooking is complete, the fish should be cooked through and the potatoes crispy outside and tender inside. Serve hot with tartar sauce, cocktail sauce, or malt vinegar (if using).

Nutrition:

- (Per serving) Calories: 360; Total fat: 8g; Saturated fat: 1g; Carbohydrates: 40g; Fiber: 2g; Protein: 30g; Sodium: 302mg

Steamed Cod With Garlic And Swiss Chard

Servings: 4
Cooking Time: 12 Minutes
Ingredients:

- 1 teaspoon salt
- 1/2 teaspoon dried oregano
- 1/2 teaspoon dried thyme
- 1/2 teaspoon garlic powder
- 4 cod fillets
- 1/2 white onion, thinly sliced
- 135 g Swiss chard, washed, stemmed, and torn into pieces
- 60 ml olive oil
- 1 lemon, quartered

Directions:

1. Preheat the air fryer to 192°C.
2. In a small bowl, whisk together the salt, oregano, thyme, and garlic powder.
3. Tear off four pieces of aluminum foil, with each sheet being large enough to envelop one cod fillet and a quarter of the vegetables.
4. Place a cod fillet in the middle of each sheet of foil, then sprinkle on all sides with the spice mixture.
5. In each foil packet, place a quarter of the onion slices and 30 g Swiss chard, then drizzle 1 tablespoon olive oil and squeeze 1/4 lemon over the contents of each foil packet.
6. Fold and seal the sides of the foil packets and then place them into the two air fryer drawers. Steam for 12 minutes.
7. Remove from the drawers, and carefully open each packet to avoid a steam burn.

Sole And Cauliflower Fritters And Prawn Bake

Servings: 6
Cooking Time: 24 Minutes

Ingredients:

- Sole and Cauliflower Fritters:
- 230 g sole fillets
- 230 g mashed cauliflower
- 75 g red onion, chopped
- 1 bell pepper, finely chopped
- 1 egg, beaten
- 2 garlic cloves, minced
- 2 tablespoons fresh parsley, chopped
- 1 tablespoon olive oil
- 1 tablespoon coconut aminos or tamari
- ½ teaspoon scotch bonnet pepper, minced
- ½ teaspoon paprika
- Salt and white pepper, to taste
- Cooking spray
- Prawn Bake:
- 400 g prawns, peeled and deveined
- 1 egg, beaten
- 120 ml coconut milk
- 120 g Cheddar cheese, shredded
- ½ teaspoon coconut oil
- 1 teaspoon ground coriander

Directions:

1. Make the Sole and Cauliflower Fritters :
2. 1. Preheat the air fryer to 200°C. Spray the zone 1 air fryer basket with cooking spray. Place the sole fillets in the basket and air fry for 10 minutes, flipping them halfway through. 3. When the fillets are done, transfer them to a large bowl. Mash the fillets into flakes. Add the remaining ingredients and stir to combine. 4. Make the fritters: Scoop out 2 tablespoons of the fish mixture and shape into a patty about ½ inch thick with your hands. Repeat with the remaining fish mixture. 5. Arrange the patties in the zone 1 air fryer basket and bake for 14 minutes, flipping the patties halfway through, or until they are golden brown and cooked through. 6. Cool for 5 minutes and serve on a plate.
3. Make the Prawn Bake :
4. In the mixing bowl, mix prawns with egg, coconut milk, Cheddar cheese, coconut oil, and ground coriander.
5. Then put the mixture in the baking ramekins and put in the zone 2 air fryer basket.
6. Cook the prawns at 205°C for 5 minutes.

Fish And Chips

Servings:2
Cooking Time:22

Ingredients:

- 1 pound of potatoes, cut lengthwise
- 1 cup seasoned flour
- 2 eggs, organic
- 1/3 cup buttermilk
- 2 cup seafood fry mix
- ½ cup bread crumbs
- 2 codfish fillet, 6 ounces each
- Oil spray, for greasing

Directions:

1. take a bowl and whisk eggs in it along buttermilk.
2. In a separate bowl mix seafood fry mix and bread crumbs
3. Take a baking tray and spread flour on it
4. Dip the fillets first in egg wash, then in flour, and at the end coat it with breadcrumbs mixture.
5. Put the fish fillet in air fryer zone 1 basket.
6. Grease the fish fillet with oil spray.
7. Set zone 1 to AIR FRY mode at 400 degrees F for 14 minutes.
8. Put potato chip in zone two baskets and lightly grease it with oil spray.
9. Set the zone 2 basket to AIRFRY mode at 400 degrees F for 22 minutes.
10. Hit the smart finish button.
11. Once done, serve and enjoy.

Nutrition:

- (Per serving) Calories 992| Fat 22.3g| Sodium1406 mg | Carbs 153.6g | Fiber 10g | Sugar10 g | Protein 40g

Lemony Prawns And Courgette

Servings: 4

Cooking Time: 7 To 8 Minutes

Ingredients:

- 570 g extra-large raw prawns, peeled and deveined
- 2 medium courgettes (about 230 g each), halved lengthwise and cut into ½-inch-thick slices
- 1½ tablespoons olive oil
- ½ teaspoon garlic salt
- 1½ teaspoons dried oregano
- ⅛ teaspoon crushed red pepper flakes (optional)
- Juice of ½ lemon
- 1 tablespoon chopped fresh mint
- 1 tablespoon chopped fresh dill

Directions:

1. Preheat the air fryer to 176°C.
2. In a large bowl, combine the prawns, courgette, oil, garlic salt, oregano, and pepper flakes and toss to coat.
3. Arrange a single layer of the prawns and courgette in the two air fryer drawers. Air fry for 7 to 8 minutes, shaking the drawer halfway, until the courgette is golden and the prawns are cooked through.
4. Transfer to a serving dish and tent with foil while you air fry the remaining prawns and courgette.
5. Top with the lemon juice, mint, and dill and serve.

Tandoori Prawns

Servings: 4

Cooking Time: 6 Minutes

Ingredients:

- 455 g jumbo raw prawns (21 to 25 count), peeled and deveined
- 1 tablespoon minced fresh ginger
- 3 cloves garlic, minced
- 5 g chopped fresh coriander or parsley, plus more for garnish
- 1 teaspoon ground turmeric
- 1 teaspoon garam masala
- 1 teaspoon smoked paprika
- 1 teaspoon kosher or coarse sea salt
- ½ to 1 teaspoon cayenne pepper
- 2 tablespoons olive oil (for Paleo) or melted ghee
- 2 teaspoons fresh lemon juice

Directions:

1. In a large bowl, combine the prawns, ginger, garlic, coriander, turmeric, garam masala, paprika, salt, and cayenne. Toss well to coat. Add the oil or ghee and toss again. Marinate at room temperature for 15 minutes, or cover and refrigerate for up to 8 hours.
2. Place the prawns in a single layer in the two air fryer baskets. Set the air fryer to 165°C for 6 minutes. Transfer the prawns to a serving platter. Cover and let the prawns finish cooking in the residual heat, about 5 minutes.
3. Sprinkle the prawns with the lemon juice and toss to coat. Garnish with additional cilantro and serve.

Crispy Catfish

Servings: 4

Cooking Time: 17 Minutes

Ingredients:

- 4 catfish fillets
- ¼ cup Louisiana Fish fry
- 1 tablespoon olive oil
- 1 tablespoon parsley, chopped
- 1 lemon, sliced
- Fresh herbs, to garnish

Directions:

1. Mix fish fry with olive oil, and parsley then liberally rub over the catfish.
2. Place two fillets in each of the crisper plate.
3. Return the crisper plates to the Tefal Dual Zone Air Fryer.
4. Choose the Air Fry mode for Zone 1 and set the temperature to 390 degrees F and the time to 17 minutes|
5. Select the "MATCH" button to copy the settings for Zone 2.
6. Initiate cooking by pressing the START/STOP button.
7. Garnish with lemon slices and herbs.
8. Serve warm.

Shrimp With Lemon And Pepper

Servings: 4

Cooking Time: 8 Minutes

Ingredients:

- 455g raw shrimp, peeled and deveined
- 118ml olive oil
- 2 tablespoons lemon juice
- 1 teaspoon black pepper
- ½ teaspoon salt

Directions:

1. Toss shrimp with black pepper, salt, lemon juice and oil in a bowl.
2. Divide the shrimp into the Tefal 2 Baskets Air Fryer baskets.
3. Return the air fryer basket 1 to Zone 1, and basket 2 to Zone 2 of the Tefal 2-Basket Air Fryer.
4. Choose the "Air Fry" mode for Zone 1 at 350 degrees F and 8 minutes of cooking time.
5. Select the "MATCH COOK" option to copy the settings for Zone 2.
6. Initiate cooking by pressing the START/PAUSE BUTTON.
7. Serve warm.

Nutrition:

- (Per serving) Calories 257 | Fat 10.4g |Sodium 431mg | Carbs 20g | Fiber 0g | Sugar 1.6g | Protein 21g

Simple Buttery Cod & Salmon On Bed Of Fennel And Carrot

Servings: 4

Cooking Time: 13 To 14 Minutes

Ingredients:

- Simple Buttery Cod:
- 2 cod fillets, 110 g each
- 2 tablespoons salted butter, melted
- 1 teaspoon Old Bay seasoning
- ½ medium lemon, sliced
- Salmon on Bed of Fennel and Carrot:
- 1 fennel bulb, thinly sliced
- 1 large carrot, peeled and sliced
- 1 small onion, thinly sliced
- 60 ml low-fat sour cream
- ¼ teaspoon coarsely ground pepper
- 2 salmon fillets, 140 g each

Directions:

1. Make the Simple Buttery Cod :
2. Place cod fillets into a round baking dish. Brush each fillet with butter and sprinkle with Old Bay seasoning. Lay two lemon slices on each fillet. Cover the dish with foil and place into the zone 1 air fryer basket.
3. Adjust the temperature to 175°C and bake for 8 minutes. Flip halfway through the cooking time. When cooked, internal temperature should be at least 65°C. Serve warm.
4. Make the Salmon on Bed of Fennel and Carrot :
5. Combine the fennel, carrot, and onion in a bowl and toss.
6. Put the vegetable mixture into a baking pan. Roast in the zone 2 air fryer basket at 205°C for 4 minutes or until the vegetables are crisp-tender.
7. Remove the pan from the air fryer. Stir in the sour cream and sprinkle the vegetables with the pepper.
8. Top with the salmon fillets.
9. Return the pan to the air fryer. Roast for another 9 to 10 minutes or until the salmon just barely flakes when tested with a fork.

Salmon With Green Beans

Servings:1

Cooking Time:18

Ingredients:

- 1 salmon fillet, 2 inches thick
- 2 teaspoons of olive oil
- 2 teaspoons of smoked paprika
- Salt and black pepper, to taste
- 1 cup green beans
- Oil spray, for greasing

Directions:

1. Grease the green beans with oil spray and add them to zone 1 basket.
2. Now rub the salmon fillet with olive oil, smoked paprika, salt, and black pepper.
3. Put the salmon fillets in the zone 2 basket.
4. Now set the zone one basket to AIRFRY mode at 350 degrees F for 18 minutes.
5. Set the Zone 2 basket to 390 degrees F for 16-18 minutes
6. Hit the smart finish button.
7. Once done, take out the salmon and green beans and transfer them to the serving plates and enjoy.

Nutrition:

- (Per serving) Calories 367| Fat22 g| Sodium 87mg | Carbs 10.2g | Fiber 5.3g | Sugar 2g | Protein 37.2g

Tuna Patties With Spicy Sriracha Sauce Coconut Prawns

Servings: 6
Cooking Time: 10 Minutes

Ingredients:

- Tuna Patties with Spicy Sriracha Sauce:
- 2 (170 g) cans tuna packed in oil, drained
- 3 tablespoons almond flour
- 2 tablespoons mayonnaise
- 1 teaspoon dried dill
- ½ teaspoon onion powder
- Pinch of salt and pepper
- Spicy Sriracha Sauce:
- 60 g mayonnaise
- 1 tablespoon Sriracha sauce
- 1 teaspoon garlic powder
- Coconut Prawns:
- 230 g medium prawns, peeled and deveined
- 2 tablespoons salted butter, melted
- ½ teaspoon Old Bay seasoning
- 25 g desiccated, unsweetened coconut

Directions:

1. Make the Tuna Patties with Spicy Sriracha Sauce :
2. 1. Preheat the air fryer to 192°C. Line the zone 1 drawer with baking paper. In a large bowl, combine the tuna, almond flour, mayonnaise, dill, and onion powder. Season to taste with salt and freshly ground black pepper. Use a fork to stir, mashing with the back of the fork as necessary, until thoroughly combined. 3. Use an ice cream scoop to form the tuna mixture patties. Place the patties in a single layer on the baking paper in the zone 1 air fryer drawer. Press lightly with the bottom of the scoop to flatten into a circle about ½ inch thick. Pausing halfway through the cooking time to turn the patties, air fry for 10 minutes until lightly browned. 4. To make the Sriracha sauce: In a small bowl, combine the mayonnaise, Sriracha, and garlic powder. Serve the tuna patties topped with the Sriracha sauce.
3. Make the Coconut Prawns :
4. In a large bowl, toss the prawns in butter and Old Bay seasoning.
5. Place shredded coconut in bowl. Coat each piece of prawns in the coconut and place into the zone 2 air fryer drawer.
6. Adjust the temperature to 204°C and air fry for 6 minutes.
7. Gently turn the prawns halfway through the cooking time. Serve immediately.

Lemon Pepper Salmon With Asparagus

Servings:2
Cooking Time:18

Ingredients:

- 1 cup of green asparagus
- 2 tablespoons of butter
- 2 fillets of salmon, 8 ounces each
- Salt and black pepper, to taste
- 1 teaspoon of lemon juice
- ½ teaspoon of lemon zest
- oil spray, for greasing

Directions:

1. Rinse and trim the asparagus.
2. Rinse and pat dry the salmon fillets.
3. Take a bowl and mix lemon juice, lemon zest, salt, and black pepper.
4. Brush the fish fillet with the rub and place it in the zone 1 basket.
5. Place asparagus in zone 2 basket.
6. Spray the asparagus with oil spray.
7. Set zone 1 to AIRFRY mode for 18 minutes at 390 degrees F.
8. Set the zone 2 to 5 minutes at 390 degrees F, at air fry mode.
9. Hit the smart finish button to finish at the same time.
10. Once done, serve and enjoy.

Nutrition:

- (Per serving) Calories 482| Fat 28g| Sodium209 mg | Carbs 2.8g | Fiber1.5 g | Sugar1.4 g | Protein 56.3g

Breaded Scallops

Servings: 4
Cooking Time: 12 Minutes
Ingredients:

- ½ cup crushed buttery crackers
- ½ teaspoon garlic powder
- ½ teaspoon seafood seasoning
- 2 tablespoons butter, melted
- 1 pound sea scallops patted dry
- cooking spray

Directions:

1. Mix cracker crumbs, garlic powder, and seafood seasoning in a shallow bowl. Spread melted butter in another shallow bowl.
2. Dip each scallop in the melted butter and then roll in the breading to coat well.
3. Grease each Air fryer basket with cooking spray and place half of the scallops in each.
4. Return the crisper plate to the Tefal Dual Zone Air Fryer.
5. Select the Air Fry mode for Zone 1 and set the temperature to 390 degrees F and the time to 12 minutes|
6. Press the "MATCH" button to copy the settings for Zone 2.
7. Initiate cooking by pressing the START/STOP button.
8. Flip the scallops with a spatula after 4 minutes and resume cooking.
9. Serve warm.

Honey Teriyaki Salmon

Servings: 3
Cooking Time: 12 Minutes
Ingredients:

- 8 tablespoon teriyaki sauce
- 3 tablespoons honey
- 2 cubes frozen garlic
- 2 tablespoons olive oil
- 3 pieces wild salmon

Directions:

1. Mix teriyaki sauce, honey, garlic and oil in a large bowl.
2. Add salmon to this sauce and mix well to coat.
3. Cover and refrigerate the salmon for 20 minutes.
4. Place the salmon pieces in one air fryer basket.
5. Return the air fryer basket 1 to Zone 1 of the Tefal 2-Basket Air Fryer.
6. Choose the "Air Fry" mode for Zone 1 and set the temperature to 350 degrees F and 12 minutes of cooking time.
7. Initiate cooking by pressing the START/PAUSE BUTTON.
8. Flip the pieces once cooked halfway through.
9. Serve warm.

Nutrition:

- (Per serving) Calories 260 | Fat 16g |Sodium 585mg | Carbs 3.1g | Fiber 1.3g | Sugar 0.2g | Protein 25.5g

Butter-wine Baked Salmon

Servings: 4
Cooking Time: 10 Minutes
Ingredients:

- 4 tablespoons butter, melted
- 2 cloves garlic, minced
- Sea salt and ground black pepper, to taste
- 60 ml dry white wine or apple cider vinegar
- 1 tablespoon lime juice
- 1 teaspoon smoked paprika
- ½ teaspoon onion powder
- 4 salmon steaks
- Cooking spray

Directions:

1. Place all the ingredients except the salmon and oil in a shallow dish and stir to mix well.
2. Add the salmon steaks, turning to coat well on both sides. Transfer the salmon to the refrigerator to marinate for 30 minutes.
3. Preheat the air fryer to 182°C.
4. Place the salmon steaks in the two air fryer drawers, discarding any excess marinade. Spray the salmon steaks with cooking spray.
5. Air fry for about 10 minutes, flipping the salmon steaks halfway through, or until cooked to your preferred doneness.
6. Divide the salmon steaks among four plates and serve.

Bang Bang Shrimp With Roasted Bok Choy

Servings:4
Cooking Time: 13 Minutes
Ingredients:

- FOR THE BANG BANG SHRIMP
- ½ cup all-purpose flour
- 2 large eggs
- 1 cup panko bread crumbs
- 1 pound peeled shrimp (tails removed), thawed if frozen
- Nonstick cooking spray
- ½ cup mayonnaise
- ¼ cup Thai sweet chili sauce
- ¼ teaspoon sriracha
- FOR THE BOK CHOY
- 1 tablespoon reduced-sodium soy sauce
- 1 teaspoon minced garlic
- 1 teaspoon sesame oil
- 1 teaspoon minced fresh ginger
- 1½ pounds baby bok choy, halved lengthwise
- 1 tablespoon toasted sesame seeds

Directions:

1. To prep the shrimp: Set up a breading station with three small shallow bowls. Place the flour in the first bowl. In the second bowl, whisk the eggs. Place the panko in the third bowl.
2. Bread the shrimp in this order: First, dip them into the flour, coating both sides. Then, dip into the beaten egg. Finally, coat them in the panko, gently pressing the bread crumbs to adhere to the shrimp. Spritz both sides of the shrimp with cooking spray.
3. To prep the bok choy: In a small bowl, whisk together the soy sauce, garlic, sesame oil, and ginger.
4. To cook the shrimp and bok choy: Install a crisper plate in the Zone 1 basket. Place the shrimp in the basket in a single layer and insert the basket in the unit. Place the boy choy cut-side up in the Zone 2 basket. Pour the sauce over the bok choy and insert the basket in the unit.
5. Select Zone 1, select AIR FRY, set the temperature to 390°F, and set the timer to 13 minutes.
6. Select Zone 2, select BAKE, set the temperature to 370°F, and set the timer to 8 minutes. Select SMART FINISH.
7. Press START/PAUSE to begin cooking.
8. When cooking is complete, the shrimp should be cooked through and golden brown and the bok choy soft and slightly caramelized.
9. In a large bowl, whisk together the mayonnaise, sweet chili sauce, and sriracha. Add the shrimp and toss to coat.
10. Sprinkle the bok choy with the sesame seeds and serve hot alongside the shrimp.

Nutrition:

- (Per serving) Calories: 534; Total fat: 33g; Saturated fat: 4g; Carbohydrates: 29g; Fiber: 3g; Protein: 31g; Sodium: 789mg

Garlic Butter Salmon

Servings: 4
Cooking Time: 10 Minutes
Ingredients:

- 4 (6-ounce) boneless, skin-on salmon fillets (preferably wild-caught)
- 4 tablespoons butter, melted
- 2 teaspoons garlic, minced
- 2 teaspoons fresh Italian parsley, chopped (or ¼ teaspoon dried)
- Salt and pepper to taste

Directions:

1. Season the fresh salmon with salt and pepper.
2. Mix together the melted butter, garlic, and parsley in a bowl.
3. Baste the salmon fillets with the garlic butter mixture.
4. Place a crisper plate in each drawer. Put 2 fillets in each drawer. Put the drawers inside the unit.
5. Select zone 1, then AIR FRY, then set the temperature to 360 degrees F/ 180 degrees C with a 10-minute timer. To match zone 2 settings to zone 1, choose MATCH. To begin, select START/STOP.
6. Remove the salmon from the drawers after the timer has finished.

Nutrition:

- (Per serving) Calories 338 | Fat 26g | Sodium 309mg | Carbs 1g | Fiber 0g | Sugar 0g | Protein 25g

Poultry Recipes

Nice Goulash

Servings: 2
Cooking Time: 17 Minutes
Ingredients:

- 2 red bell peppers, chopped
- 450 g chicken mince
- 2 medium tomatoes, diced
- 120 ml chicken broth
- Salt and ground black pepper, to taste
- Cooking spray

Directions:

1. Preheat the zone 1 air fryer drawer to 186°C. Spritz a baking pan with cooking spray.
2. Set the bell pepper in the baking pan and put in the zone 1 air fry drawer to broil for 5 minutes or until the bell pepper is tender. Shake the drawer halfway through.
3. Add the chicken mince and diced tomatoes in the baking pan and stir to mix well. Broil for 6 more minutes or until the chicken is lightly browned.
4. Pour the chicken broth over and sprinkle with salt and ground black pepper. Stir to mix well. Broil for an additional 6 minutes.
5. Serve immediately.

Bacon Wrapped Stuffed Chicken

Servings: 4
Cooking Time: 25 Minutes
Ingredients:

- 3 boneless chicken breasts
- 6 jalapenos, sliced
- ¾ cup (170g) cream cheese
- ½ cup Monterey Jack cheese, shredded
- 1 teaspoon ground cumin
- 12 strips thick bacon

Directions:

1. Cut the chicken breasts in half crosswise and pound them with a mallet.
2. Mix cream cheese with cumin and Monterey jacket cheese in a bowl.
3. Spread the cream cheese mixture over the chicken breast slices.
4. Add jalapeno slices on top and wrap the chicken slices.
5. Wrap each chicken rolls with a bacon slice.
6. Place the wrapped rolls into the Tefal 2 Baskets Air Fryer baskets.
7. Return the air fryer basket 1 to Zone 1, and basket 2 to Zone 2 of the Tefal 2-Basket Air Fryer.
8. Choose the "Air Fry" mode for Zone 1 at 340 degrees F and 25 minutes of cooking time.
9. Select the "MATCH COOK" option to copy the settings for Zone 2.
10. Initiate cooking by pressing the START/PAUSE BUTTON.
11. Serve warm.

Nutrition:

- (Per serving) Calories 220 | Fat 1.7g |Sodium 178mg | Carbs 1.7g | Fiber 0.2g | Sugar 0.2g | Protein 32.9g

Chicken With Bacon And Tomato

Servings: 4
Cooking Time: 10 Minutes
Ingredients:

- 4 medium-sized skin-on chicken drumsticks
- 1½ teaspoons herbs de Provence
- Salt and pepper, to taste
- 1 tablespoon rice vinegar
- 2 tablespoons olive oil
- 2 garlic cloves, crushed
- 340 g crushed canned tomatoes
- 1 small-size leek, thinly sliced
- 2 slices smoked bacon, chopped

Directions:

1. Sprinkle the chicken drumsticks with herbs de Provence, salt and pepper; then, drizzle them with rice vinegar and olive oil.
2. Cook in the baking pan at 180°C for 8 to 10 minutes. Pause the air fryer; stir in the remaining ingredients and continue to cook for 15 minutes longer; make sure to check them periodically. Bon appétit!

Garlic, Buffalo, And Blue Cheese Stuffed Chicken

Servings: 2
Cooking Time: 30 Minutes

Ingredients:

- ¼ teaspoon garlic powder
- ¼ teaspoon onion powder
- ¼ teaspoon paprika
- 2 boneless, skinless chicken breasts
- ½ tablespoon canola oil
- 2 ounces softened cream cheese
- ¼ cup shredded cheddar cheese
- ¼ cup blue cheese crumbles
- ¼ cup buffalo sauce
- 1 tablespoon dry ranch seasoning
- 2 tablespoons dried chives
- 1 tablespoon minced garlic
- Optional toppings:
- Ranch dressing
- Buffalo sauce
- Fresh parsley

Directions:

1. Combine the garlic powder, onion powder, and paprika in a small bowl.
2. Drizzle the chicken breasts with oil and season evenly with the garlic powder mixture on a cutting board.
3. Make a deep pocket in the center of each chicken breast, but be cautious not to cut all the way through.
4. Combine the remaining ingredients in a medium mixing bowl and stir until thoroughly blended. Fill each chicken breast's pocket with the cream cheese mixture.
5. Place the chicken in both drawers and insert both drawers into the unit. Select zone 1, then BAKE, and set the temperature to 375 degrees F/ 190 degrees C with a 30-minute timer. To match zone 2 and zone 1 settings, select MATCH. To start cooking, use the START/STOP button.
6. Garnish the cooked chicken with ranch dressing, spicy sauce, and parsley on top.

Nutrition:

- (Per serving) Calories 369 | Fat 23.8g | Sodium 568mg | Carbs 4.3g | Fiber 0.4g | Sugar 0.5g | Protein 34.7g

Chicken Drumettes

Servings: 5
Cooking Time: 52 Minutes

Ingredients:

- 10 large chicken drumettes
- Cooking spray
- ¼ cup of rice vinegar
- 3 tablespoons honey
- 2 tablespoons unsalted chicken stock
- 1 tablespoon soy sauce
- 1 tablespoon toasted sesame oil
- ⅜ teaspoons crushed red pepper
- 1 garlic clove, chopped
- 2 tablespoons chopped unsalted roasted peanuts
- 1 tablespoon chopped fresh chives

Directions:

1. Spread the chicken in the two crisper plates in an even layer and spray cooking spray on top.
2. Return the crisper plate to the Tefal Dual Zone Air Fryer.
3. Choose the Air Fry mode for Zone 1 and set the temperature to 390 degrees F and the time to 47 minutes|
4. Select the "MATCH" button to copy the settings for Zone 2.
5. Initiate cooking by pressing the START/STOP button.
6. Flip the chicken drumettes once cooked halfway through, then resume cooking.
7. During this time, mix soy sauce, honey, stock, vinegar, garlic, and crushed red pepper in a suitable saucepan and place it over medium-high heat to cook on a simmer.
8. Cook this sauce for 6 minutes with occasional stirring, then pour it into a medium-sized bowl.
9. Add air fried drumettes and toss well to coat with the honey sauce.
10. Garnish with chives and peanuts.
11. Serve warm and fresh.

Almond Chicken

Servings: 4

Cooking Time: 25 Minutes

Ingredients:

- 2 large eggs
- ½ cup buttermilk
- 2 teaspoons garlic salt
- 1 teaspoon pepper
- 2 cups slivered almonds, finely chopped
- 4 boneless, skinless chicken breast halves (6 ounces each)

Directions:

1. Whisk together the egg, buttermilk, garlic salt, and pepper in a small bowl.
2. In another small bowl, place the almonds.
3. Dip the chicken in the egg mixture, then roll it in the almonds, patting it down to help the coating stick.
4. Install a crisper plate in both drawers. Place half the chicken breasts in the zone 1 drawer and half in zone 2's, then insert the drawers into the unit.
5. Select zone 1, select AIR FRY, set temperature to 390 degrees F/ 200 degrees C, and set time to 22 minutes. Select MATCH to match zone 2 settings to zone 1. Press the START/STOP button to begin cooking.
6. When the time reaches 11 minutes, press START/STOP to pause the unit. Remove the drawers and flip the chicken. Re-insert the drawers into the unit and press START/STOP to resume cooking.
7. When cooking is complete, remove the chicken.

Nutrition:

- (Per serving) Calories 353 | Fat 18g | Sodium 230mg | Carbs 6g | Fiber 2g | Sugar 3g | Protein 41g

Bang-bang Chicken

Servings: 2

Cooking Time: 20 Minutes

Ingredients:

- 1 cup mayonnaise
- ½ cup sweet chili sauce
- 2 tablespoons Sriracha sauce
- ⅓ cup flour
- 1 lb. boneless chicken breast, diced
- 1 ½ cups panko bread crumbs
- 2 green onions, chopped

Directions:

1. Mix mayonnaise with Sriracha and sweet chili sauce in a large bowl.
2. Keep ¾ cup of the mixture aside.
3. Add flour, chicken, breadcrumbs, and remaining mayo mixture to a resealable plastic bag.
4. Zip the bag and shake well to coat.
5. Divide the chicken in the two crisper plates in a single layer.
6. Return the crisper plate to the Tefal Dual Zone Air Fryer.
7. Choose the Air Fry mode for Zone 1 and set the temperature to 390 degrees F and the time to 20 minutes|
8. Select the "MATCH" button to copy the settings for Zone 2.
9. Initiate cooking by pressing the START/STOP button.
10. Flip the chicken once cooked halfway through.
11. Top the chicken with reserved mayo sauce.
12. Garnish with green onions and serve warm.

Garlic Parmesan Drumsticks

Servings: 4

Cooking Time: 25 Minutes

Ingredients:

- 8 (115 g) chicken drumsticks
- ½ teaspoon salt
- ⅛ teaspoon ground black pepper
- ½ teaspoon garlic powder
- 2 tablespoons salted butter, melted
- 45 g grated Parmesan cheese
- 1 tablespoon dried parsley

Directions:

1. Sprinkle drumsticks with salt, pepper, and garlic powder. Place drumsticks into the two ungreased air fryer baskets.
2. Adjust the temperature to 200°C and air fry for 25 minutes, turning drumsticks halfway through cooking. Drumsticks will be golden and have an internal temperature of at least 75°C when done.
3. Transfer drumsticks to a large serving dish. Pour butter over drumsticks, and sprinkle with Parmesan and parsley. Serve warm.

Stuffed Chicken Florentine

Servings: 4
Cooking Time: 20 Minutes
Ingredients:

- 3 tablespoons pine nuts
- 40 g frozen spinach, thawed and squeezed dry
- 75 g ricotta cheese
- 2 tablespoons grated Parmesan cheese
- 3 cloves garlic, minced
- Salt and freshly ground black pepper, to taste
- 4 small boneless, skinless chicken breast halves (about 680 g)
- 8 slices bacon

Directions:

1. In a large bowl, combine the spinach, ricotta, Parmesan, and garlic. Season to taste with salt and pepper and stir well until thoroughly combined.
2. Using a sharp knife, cut into the chicken breasts, slicing them across and opening them up like a book, but be careful not to cut them all the way through. Sprinkle the chicken with salt and pepper.
3. Spoon equal amounts of the spinach mixture into the chicken, then fold the top of the chicken breast back over the top of the stuffing. Wrap each chicken breast with 2 slices of bacon.
4. Air fry the chicken for 18 to 20 minutes in zone 1 drawer until the bacon is crisp and a thermometer inserted into the thickest part of the chicken registers 76°C.
5. Place the pine nuts in a small pan and set in the zone 2 air fryer drawer. Air fry at 200°C for 2 to 3 minutes until toasted. Remove the pine nuts to a mixing bowl.

Harissa-rubbed Chicken

Servings: 4
Cooking Time: 21 Minutes
Ingredients:

- Harissa:
- 120 ml olive oil
- 6 cloves garlic, minced
- 2 tablespoons smoked paprika
- 1 tablespoon ground coriander
- 1 tablespoon ground cumin
- 1 teaspoon ground caraway
- 1 teaspoon kosher salt
- ½ to 1 teaspoon cayenne pepper
- Chickens:
- 120 g yogurt
- 2 small chickens, any giblets removed, split in half lengthwise

Directions:

1. For the harissa: In a medium microwave-safe bowl, combine the oil, garlic, paprika, coriander, cumin, caraway, salt, and cayenne. Microwave on high for 1 minute, stirring halfway through the cooking time. 2. For the chicken: In a small bowl, combine 1 to 2 tablespoons harissa and the yogurt. Whisk until well combined. Place the chicken halves in a resealable plastic bag and pour the marinade over. Seal the bag and massage until all of the pieces are thoroughly coated. Marinate at room temperature for 30 minutes or in the refrigerator for up to 24 hours. 3. Arrange the hen halves in a single layer in the two air fryer drawers. Set the air fryer to 200°C for 20 minutes. Use a meat thermometer to ensure the chickens have reached an internal temperature of 76°C.

Juicy Duck Breast

Servings: 1
Cooking Time: 20 Minutes
Ingredients:

- ½ duck breast
- Salt and black pepper, to taste
- 2 tablespoons plum sauce

Directions:

1. Rub the duck breast with black pepper and salt.
2. Place the duck breast in air fryer basket 1 and add plum sauce on top.
3. Return the basket to the Tefal 2 Baskets Air Fryer.
4. Choose the "Air Fry" mode for Zone 1 and set the temperature to 400 degrees F and 20 minutes of cooking time.
5. Initiate cooking by pressing the START/PAUSE BUTTON.
6. Flip the duck breast once cooked halfway through.
7. Serve warm.

Nutrition:

- (Per serving) Calories 379 | Fat 19g |Sodium 184mg | Carbs 12.3g | Fiber 0.6g | Sugar 2g | Protein 37.7g

Broccoli Cheese Chicken

Servings: 4
Cooking Time: 25 Minutes
Ingredients:

- 1 tablespoon avocado oil
- 15 g chopped onion
- 35 g finely chopped broccoli
- 115 g cream cheese, at room temperature
- 60 g Cheddar cheese, shredded
- 1 teaspoon garlic powder
- ½ teaspoon sea salt, plus additional for seasoning, divided
- ¼ freshly ground black pepper, plus additional for seasoning, divided
- 900 g boneless, skinless chicken breasts
- 1 teaspoon smoked paprika

Directions:

1. Heat a medium skillet over medium-high heat and pour in the avocado oil. Add the onion and broccoli and cook, stirring occasionally, for 5 to 8 minutes, until the onion is tender.
2. Transfer to a large bowl and stir in the cream cheese, Cheddar cheese, and garlic powder, and season to taste with salt and pepper.
3. Hold a sharp knife parallel to the chicken breast and cut a long pocket into one side. Stuff the chicken pockets with the broccoli mixture, using toothpicks to secure the pockets around the filling.
4. In a small dish, combine the paprika, ½ teaspoon salt, and ¼ teaspoon pepper. Sprinkle this over the outside of the chicken.
5. Set the air fryer to 200°C. Place the chicken in a single layer in the two air fryer drawers and cook for 14 to 16 minutes, until an instant-read thermometer reads 70°C. Place the chicken on a plate and tent a piece of aluminum foil over the chicken. Allow to rest for 5 to 10 minutes before serving.

Air-fried Turkey Breast With Roasted Green Bean Casserole

Servings: 4
Cooking Time: 50 Minutes
Ingredients:

- FOR THE TURKEY BREAST
- 2 teaspoons unsalted butter, at room temperature
- 1 bone-in split turkey breast (3 pounds), thawed if frozen
- 1 teaspoon poultry seasoning
- ½ teaspoon kosher salt
- ⅓ teaspoon freshly ground black pepper
- FOR THE GREEN BEAN CASSEROLE
- 1 (10.5-ounce) can condensed cream of mushroom soup
- ½ cup whole milk
- 1 cup store-bought crispy fried onions, divided
- ¼ teaspoon kosher salt
- ¼ teaspoon freshly ground black pepper
- 1 pound green beans, trimmed
- ¼ cup panko bread crumbs
- Nonstick cooking spray

Directions:

1. To prep the turkey breast: Spread the butter over the skin side of the turkey. Season with the poultry seasoning, salt, and black pepper.
2. To prep the green bean casserole: In a medium bowl, combine the soup, milk, ½ cup of crispy onions, the salt, and black pepper.
3. To cook the turkey and beans:
4. Install a crisper plate in the Zone 1 basket. Place the turkey skin-side up in the basket and insert the basket in the unit. Place the green beans in the Zone 2 basket and insert the basket in the unit.
5. Select Zone 1, select AIR FRY, set the temperature to 360°F, and set the time to 50 minutes.
6. Select Zone 2, select ROAST, set the temperature to 350°F, and set the time to 40 minutes. Select SMART FINISH.
7. Press START/PAUSE to begin cooking.
8. When the Zone 2 timer reads 30 minutes, press START/PAUSE. Remove the basket and stir the soup mixture into the beans. Scatter the panko and remaining ½ cup of crispy onions over the top, then spritz with cooking spray. Reinsert the basket and press START/PAUSE to resume cooking.
9. When cooking is complete, the turkey will be cooked through and the green bean casserole will be bubbling and golden brown on top.
10. Let the turkey and casserole rest for at least 15 minutes before serving.
11. Per serving
12. Calories: 577| Total fat: 22g| Saturated fat: 6.5g| Carbohydrates: 24g| Fiber: 3.5g| Protein: 68g| Sodium: 1,165mg

Chicken And Potatoes

Servings: 2
Cooking Time: 10 Minutes
Ingredients:

- 2 potatoes, diced
- 2 chicken breasts, diced
- 4 cloves garlic crushed
- 2 teaspoons smoked paprika
- ½ teaspoon red chili flakes
- 1 teaspoon fresh thyme
- 1 teaspoon salt
- ¼ teaspoon black pepper
- 2 tablespoons olive oil

Directions:

1. Rub chicken with half of the salt, black pepper, oil, thyme, red chili flakes, paprika and garlic.
2. Mix potatoes with remaining spices, oil and garlic in a bowl.
3. Add chicken to one air fryer basket and potatoes the second basket.
4. Return the air fryer basket 1 to Zone 1, and basket 2 to Zone 2 of the Tefal 2-Basket Air Fryer.
5. Choose the "Air Fry" mode for Zone 1 at 375 degrees F and 10 minutes of cooking time.
6. Select the "MATCH COOK" option to copy the settings for Zone 2.
7. Initiate cooking by pressing the START/PAUSE BUTTON.
8. Flip the chicken and toss potatoes once cooked halfway through.
9. Garnish with chopped parsley.
10. Serve chicken with the potatoes.

Nutrition:

- (Per serving) Calories 374 | Fat 13g |Sodium 552mg | Carbs 25g | Fiber 1.2g | Sugar 1.2g | Protein 37.7g

Veggie Stuffed Chicken Breasts

Servings: 2
Cooking Time: 10 Minutes
Ingredients:

- 4 teaspoons chili powder
- 4 teaspoons ground cumin
- 1 skinless, boneless chicken breast
- 2 teaspoons chipotle flakes
- 2 teaspoons Mexican oregano
- Salt and black pepper, to taste
- ½ red bell pepper, julienned
- ½ onion, julienned
- 1 fresh jalapeno pepper, julienned
- 2 teaspoons corn oil
- ½ lime, juiced

Directions:

1. Slice the chicken breast in half horizontally.
2. Pound each chicken breast with a mallet into ¼ inch thickness.
3. Rub the pounded chicken breast with black pepper, salt, oregano, chipotle flakes, cumin, and chili powder.
4. Add ½ of bell pepper, jalapeno, and onion on top of each chicken breast piece.
5. Roll the chicken to wrap the filling inside and insert toothpicks to seal.
6. Place the rolls in crisper plate and spray them with cooking oil.
7. Return the crisper plate to the Tefal Dual Zone Air Fryer.
8. Choose the Air Fry mode for Zone 1 and set the temperature to 360 degrees F and the time to 10 minutes|
9. Initiate cooking by pressing the START/STOP button.
10. Serve warm.

Cracked-pepper Chicken Wings

Servings: 4
Cooking Time: 20 Minutes
Ingredients:

- 450 g chicken wings
- 3 tablespoons vegetable oil
- 60 g all-purpose flour
- ½ teaspoon smoked paprika
- ½ teaspoon garlic powder
- ½ teaspoon kosher salt
- 1½ teaspoons freshly cracked black pepper

Directions:

1. Place the chicken wings in a large bowl. Drizzle the vegetable oil over wings and toss to coat.
2. In a separate bowl, whisk together the flour, paprika, garlic powder, salt, and pepper until combined.
3. Dredge the wings in the flour mixture one at a time, coating them well, and place in the zone 1 air fryer drawer. Set the temperature to 200°C for 20 minutes, turning the wings halfway through the cooking time, until the breading is browned and crunchy.

Chicken Thighs With Brussels Sprouts

Servings:2
Cooking Time:30

Ingredients:

- 2 tablespoons of honey
- 4 tablespoons of Dijon mustard
- Salt and black pepper, to tat
- 4 tablespoons of olive oil
- 1-1/2 cup Brussels sprouts
- 8 chicken thighs, skinless

Directions:

1. Take a bowl and add chicken thighs to it.
2. Add honey, Dijon mustard, salt, pepper, and 2 tablespoons of olive oil to the thighs.
3. Coat the chicken well and marinate it for 1 hour.
4. Now when start cooking season the Brussels sprouts with salt and black pepper along with remaining olive oil.
5. Put the chicken in the zone 1 basket.
6. Put the Brussels sprouts into the zone 2 basket.
7. Select ROAST function for chicken and set time to 30 minutes at 390 degrees F.
8. Select AIR FRY function for Brussels sprouts and set the timer to 20 at 400 degrees F.
9. Once done, serve and enjoy.

Nutrition:

- (Per serving) Calories1454 | Fat 72.2g| Sodium 869mg | Carbs 23g | Fiber 2.7g | Sugar 19g | Protein 172g

Chicken With Bacon And Tomato & Bacon-wrapped Stuffed Chicken Breasts

Servings: 8
Cooking Time: 30 Minutes

Ingredients:

- Chicken with Bacon and Tomato:
- 4 medium-sized skin-on chicken drumsticks
- 1½ teaspoons herbs de Provence
- Salt and pepper, to taste
- 1 tablespoon rice vinegar
- 2 tablespoons olive oil
- 2 garlic cloves, crushed
- 340 g crushed canned tomatoes
- 1 small-size leek, thinly sliced
- 2 slices smoked bacon, chopped
- Bacon-Wrapped Stuffed Chicken Breasts:
- 80 g chopped frozen spinach, thawed and squeezed dry
- 55 g cream cheese, softened
- 20 g grated Parmesan cheese
- 1 jalapeño, seeded and chopped
- ½ teaspoon kosher salt
- 1 teaspoon black pepper
- 2 large boneless, skinless chicken breasts, butterflied and pounded to ½-inch thickness
- 4 teaspoons salt-free Cajun seasoning
- 6 slices bacon

Directions:

1. Make the Chicken with Bacon and Tomato :
2. Sprinkle the chicken drumsticks with herbs de Provence, salt and pepper; then, drizzle them with rice vinegar and olive oil.
3. Place into a baking pan and cook in the zone 1 basket at 180°C for 8 to 10 minutes. Pause the air fryer; stir in the remaining ingredients and continue to cook for 15 minutes longer; make sure to check them periodically. Bon appétit!
4. Make the Bacon-Wrapped Stuffed Chicken Breasts :
5. In a small bowl, combine the spinach, cream cheese, Parmesan cheese, jalapeño, salt, and pepper. Stir until well combined.
6. Place the butterflied chicken breasts on a flat surface. Spread the cream cheese mixture evenly across each piece of chicken. Starting with the narrow end, roll up each chicken breast, ensuring the filling stays inside. Season chicken with the Cajun seasoning, patting it in to ensure it sticks to the meat.
7. Wrap each breast in 3 slices of bacon. Place in the zone 2 air fryer basket. Set the air fryer to 180°C for 30 minutes. Use a meat thermometer to ensure the chicken has reached an internal temperature of 75°C.
8. Let the chicken stand 5 minutes before slicing each rolled-up breast in half to serve.

Thai Chicken With Cucumber And Chili Salad

Servings: 6
Cooking Time: 25 Minutes
Ingredients:

- 2 (570 g) small chickens, giblets discarded
- 1 tablespoon fish sauce
- 6 tablespoons chopped fresh coriander
- 2 teaspoons lime zest
- 1 teaspoon ground coriander
- 2 garlic cloves, minced
- 2 tablespoons packed light brown sugar
- 2 teaspoons vegetable oil
- Salt and ground black pepper, to taste
- 1 English cucumber, halved lengthwise and sliced thin
- 1 Thai chili, stemmed, deseeded, and minced
- 2 tablespoons chopped dry-roasted peanuts
- 1 small shallot, sliced thinly
- 1 tablespoon lime juice
- Lime wedges, for serving
- Cooking spray

Directions:

1. Arrange a chicken on a clean work surface, remove the backbone with kitchen shears, then pound the chicken breast to flat. Cut the breast in half. Repeat with the remaining chicken.
2. Loose the breast and thigh skin with your fingers, then pat the chickens dry and pierce about 10 holes into the fat deposits of the chickens. Tuck the wings under the chickens.
3. Combine 2 teaspoons of fish sauce, coriander, lime zest, coriander, garlic, 4 teaspoons of sugar, 1 teaspoon of vegetable oil, ½ teaspoon of salt, and ⅛ teaspoon of ground black pepper in a small bowl. Stir to mix well.
4. Rub the fish sauce mixture under the breast and thigh skin of the game chickens, then let sit for 10 minutes to marinate.
5. Preheat the air fryer to 200°C. Spritz the two air fryer baskets with cooking spray.
6. Arrange the marinated chickens in the preheated air fryer, skin side down.
7. Air fry for 15 minutes, then gently turn the game hens over and air fry for 10 more minutes or until the skin is golden brown and the internal temperature of the chickens reads at least 75°C.
8. Meanwhile, combine all the remaining ingredients, except for the lime wedges, in a large bowl and sprinkle with salt and black pepper. Toss to mix well.
9. Transfer the fried chickens on a large plate, then sit the salad aside and squeeze the lime wedges over before serving.

Wings With Corn On The Cob

Servings: 2
Cooking Time: 40 Minutes
Ingredients:

- 6 chicken wings, skinless
- 2 tablespoons coconut amino
- 2 tablespoons brown sugar
- 1 teaspoon ginger, paste
- ½ inch garlic, minced
- Salt and black pepper to taste
- 2 corn on cobs, small
- Oil spray, for greasing

Directions:

1. Spray the corns with oil spray and season them with salt.
2. Coat the chicken wings with coconut amino, brown sugar, ginger, garlic, salt, and black pepper.
3. Spray the wings with a good amount of oil spray.
4. Put the chicken wings in the zone 1 basket.
5. Put the corn into the zone 2 basket.
6. Select ROAST mode for the chicken wings and set the time to 23 minutes at 400 degrees F/ 200 degrees C.
7. Press 2 and select the AIR FRY mode for the corn and set the time to 40 at 300 degrees F/ 150 degrees C.
8. Once it's done, serve and enjoy.

Nutrition:

- (Per serving) Calories 950 | Fat 33.4g | Sodium 592 mg | Carbs 27.4g | Fiber 2.1g | Sugar 11.3 g | Protein 129g

Chicken And Vegetable Fajitas

Servings: 6

Cooking Time: 23 Minutes

Ingredients:

- Chicken:
- 450 g boneless, skinless chicken thighs, cut crosswise into thirds
- 1 tablespoon vegetable oil
- 4½ teaspoons taco seasoning
- Vegetables:
- 50 g sliced onion
- 150 g sliced bell pepper
- 1 or 2 jalapeños, quartered lengthwise
- 1 tablespoon vegetable oil
- ½ teaspoon kosher salt
- ½ teaspoon ground cumin
- For Serving:
- Tortillas
- Sour cream
- Shredded cheese
- Guacamole
- Salsa

Directions:

1. For the chicken: In a medium bowl, toss together the chicken, vegetable oil, and taco seasoning to coat. 2. For the vegetables: In a separate bowl, toss together the onion, bell pepper, jalapeño, vegetable oil, salt, and cumin to coat. 3. Place the chicken in the air fryer basket. Set the air fryer to (190°C for 10 minutes. Add the vegetables to the basket, toss everything together to blend the seasonings, and set the air fryer for 13 minutes more. Use a meat thermometer to ensure the chicken has reached an internal temperature of 75°C. 4. Transfer the chicken and vegetables to a serving platter. Serve with tortillas and the desired fajita fixings.

Garlic Dill Wings

Servings: 4

Cooking Time: 25 Minutes

Ingredients:

- 900 g bone-in chicken wings, separated at joints
- ½ teaspoon salt
- ½ teaspoon ground black pepper
- ½ teaspoon onion powder
- ½ teaspoon garlic powder
- 1 teaspoon dried dill

Directions:

1. In a large bowl, toss wings with salt, pepper, onion powder, garlic powder, and dill until evenly coated. Place wings into the two ungreased air fryer drawers in a single layer.
2. Adjust the temperature to 200°C and air fry for 25 minutes, shaking the drawer every 7 minutes during cooking. Wings should have an internal temperature of at least 76°C and be golden brown when done. Serve warm.

Chicken Tenders And Curly Fries

Servings: 4

Cooking Time: 35 Minutes

Ingredients:

- 1-pound frozen chicken tenders
- 1-pound frozen curly French fries
- Dipping sauces of your choice

Directions:

1. Place a crisper plate in each drawer. In the zone 1 drawer, place the chicken tenders, then place the drawer into the unit.
2. Fill the zone 2 drawer with the curly French fries, then place the drawer in the unit.
3. Select zone 1, then AIR FRY, and set the temperature to 390 degrees F/ 200 degrees C with a 22-minute timer. Select zone 2, then AIR FRY, and set the temperature to 400 degrees F/ 200 degrees C with a 30-minute timer. Select SYNC. To begin cooking, press the START/STOP button.
4. Press START/STOP to pause the device when the zone 1 and 2 times reach 8 minutes. Shake the drawers for 10 seconds after removing them from the unit. To resume cooking, re-insert the drawers into the unit and press START/STOP.
5. Enjoy!

Nutrition:

- (Per serving) Calories 500 | Fat 19.8g | Sodium 680mg | Carbs 50.1g | Fiber 4.1g | Sugar 0g | Protein 27.9g

Pickled Chicken Fillets

Servings: 4

Cooking Time: 28 Minutes

Ingredients:

- 2 boneless chicken breasts
- ½ cup dill pickle juice
- 2 eggs
- ½ cup milk
- 1 cup flour, all-purpose
- 2 tablespoons powdered sugar
- 2 tablespoons potato starch
- 1 teaspoon paprika
- 1 teaspoon of sea salt
- ½ teaspoon black pepper
- ½ teaspoon garlic powder
- ¼ teaspoon ground celery seed ground
- 1 tablespoon olive oil
- Cooking spray
- 4 hamburger buns, toasted
- 8 dill pickle chips

Directions:

1. Set the chicken in a suitable ziplock bag and pound it into ½ thickness with a mallet.
2. Slice the chicken into 2 halves.
3. Add pickle juice and seal the bag.
4. Refrigerate for 30 minutes approximately for marination. Whisk both eggs with milk in a shallow bowl.
5. Thoroughly mix flour with spices and flour in a separate bowl.
6. Dip each chicken slice in egg, then in the flour mixture.
7. Shake off the excess and set the chicken pieces in the crisper plate.
8. Spray the pieces with cooking oil.
9. Place the chicken pieces in the two crisper plate in a single layer and spray the cooking oil.
10. Return the crisper plate to the Tefal Dual Zone Air Fryer.
11. Choose the Air Fry mode for Zone 1 and set the temperature to 390 degrees F and the time to 28 minutes|
12. Select the "MATCH" button to copy the settings for Zone 2.
13. Initiate cooking by pressing the START/STOP button.
14. Flip the chicken pieces once cooked halfway through, and resume cooking.
15. Enjoy with pickle chips and a dollop of mayonnaise.

Buttermilk Fried Chicken

Servings: 6

Cooking Time: 30 Minutes

Ingredients:

- 1½ pounds boneless, skinless chicken thighs
- 2 cups buttermilk
- 1 cup all-purpose flour
- 1 tablespoon seasoned salt
- ½ tablespoon ground black pepper
- 1 cup panko breadcrumbs
- Cooking spray

Directions:

1. Place the chicken thighs in a shallow baking dish. Cover with the buttermilk. Refrigerate for 4 hours or overnight.
2. In a large gallon-sized resealable bag, combine the flour, seasoned salt, and pepper.
3. Remove the chicken from the buttermilk but don't discard the mixture.
4. Add the chicken to the bag and shake well to coat.
5. Dip the thighs in the buttermilk again, then coat in the panko breadcrumbs.
6. Install a crisper plate in each drawer. Place half the chicken thighs in the zone 1 drawer and half in zone 2's, then insert the drawers into the unit.
7. Select zone 1, select AIR FRY, set temperature to 390 degrees F/ 200 degrees C, and set time to 30 minutes. Select MATCH to match zone 2 settings to zone 1. Press the START/STOP button to begin cooking.
8. When the time reaches 15 minutes, press START/STOP to pause the unit. Remove the drawers and flip the chicken. Re-insert the drawers into the unit and press START/STOP to resume cooking.
9. When cooking is complete, remove the chicken.

Nutrition:

- (Per serving) Calories 335 | Fat 12.8g | Sodium 687mg | Carbs 33.1g | Fiber 0.4g | Sugar 4g | Protein 24.5g

Ranch Turkey Tenders With Roasted Vegetable Salad

Servings: 4
Cooking Time: 20 Minutes

Ingredients:

- FOR THE TURKEY TENDERS
- 1 pound turkey tenderloin
- ¼ cup ranch dressing
- ½ cup panko bread crumbs
- Nonstick cooking spray
- FOR THE VEGETABLE SALAD
- 1 large sweet potato, peeled and diced
- 1 zucchini, diced
- 1 red bell pepper, diced
- 1 small red onion, sliced
- 1 tablespoon vegetable oil
- ¼ teaspoon kosher salt
- ½ teaspoon freshly ground black pepper
- 2 cups baby spinach
- ½ cup store-bought balsamic vinaigrette
- ¼ cup chopped walnuts

Directions:

1. To prep the turkey tenders: Slice the turkey crosswise into 16 strips. Brush both sides of each strip with ranch dressing, then coat with the panko. Press the bread crumbs into the turkey to help them adhere. Mist both sides of the strips with cooking spray.
2. To prep the vegetables: In a large bowl, combine the sweet potato, zucchini, bell pepper, onion, and vegetable oil. Stir well to coat the vegetables. Season with the salt and black pepper.
3. To cook the turkey and vegetables:
4. Install a crisper plate in the Zone 1 basket. Place the turkey tenders in the basket in a single layer and insert the basket in the unit. Place the vegetables in the Zone 2 basket and insert the basket in the unit.
5. Select Zone 1, select AIR FRY, set the temperature to 375°F, and set the time to 20 minutes.
6. Select Zone 2, select ROAST, set the temperature to 400°F, and set the time to 20 minutes. Select SMART FINISH.
7. Press START/PAUSE to begin cooking.
8. When both timers read 10 minutes, press START/PAUSE. Remove the Zone 1 basket and use silicone-tipped tongs to flip the turkey tenders. Reinsert the basket in the unit. Remove the Zone 2 basket and shake to redistribute the vegetables. Reinsert the basket and press START/PAUSE to resume cooking.
9. When cooking is complete, the turkey will be golden brown and cooked through and the vegetables will be fork-tender.
10. Place the spinach in a large serving bowl. Mix in the roasted vegetables and balsamic vinaigrette. Sprinkle with walnuts. Serve warm with the turkey tenders.

Sweet And Spicy Carrots With Chicken Thighs

Servings:2
Cooking Time:35

Ingredients:

- Cooking spray, for greasing
- 2 tablespoons butter, melted
- 1 tablespoon hot honey
- 1 teaspoon orange zest
- 1 teaspoon cardamom
- ½ pound baby carrots
- 1 tablespoon orange juice
- Salt and black pepper, to taste
- ½ pound of carrots, baby carrots
- 8 chicken thighs

Directions:

1. Take a bowl and mix all the glaze ingredients in it.
2. Now, coat the chicken and carrots with the glaze and let it rest for 30 minutes.
3. Now place the chicken thighs into the zone 1 basket.
4. Next put the glazed carrots into the zone 2 basket.
5. Press button 1 for the first basket and set it to ROAST Mode at 350 degrees F for 35 minutes.
6. For the second basket hit 2 and set time to AIRFRY mode at 390 degrees F for 8-10 minutes.
7. Once the cooking cycle completes take out the carrots and chicken and serve it hot.

Nutrition:

- (Per serving) Calories 1312| Fat 55.4g| Sodium 757mg | Carbs 23.3g | Fiber6.7 g | Sugar12 g | Protein171 g

Maple-mustard Glazed Turkey Tenderloin With Apple And Sage Stuffing

Servings: 4
Cooking Time: 35 Minutes
Ingredients:

- FOR THE TURKEY TENDERLOIN
- 2 tablespoons maple syrup
- 1 tablespoon unsalted butter, at room temperature
- 1 tablespoon Dijon mustard
- ½ teaspoon kosher salt
- ½ teaspoon freshly ground black pepper
- 1½ pounds turkey tenderloin
- FOR THE STUFFING
- 6 ounces seasoned stuffing mix
- 1½ cups chicken broth
- 1 apple, peeled, cored, and diced
- 1 tablespoon chopped fresh sage
- 2 teaspoons unsalted butter, cut into several pieces

Directions:

1. To prep the turkey tenderloin: In a small bowl, mix the maple syrup, butter, mustard, salt, and black pepper until smooth. Spread the maple mixture over the entire turkey tenderloin.
2. To prep the stuffing: In the Zone 2 basket, combine the stuffing mix and chicken broth. Stir well to ensure the bread is fully moistened. Stir in the apple and sage. Scatter the butter on top.
3. To cook the turkey and stuffing:
4. Install a crisper plate in the Zone 1 basket. Place the turkey tenderloin in the basket and insert the basket in the unit. Insert the Zone 2 basket in the unit.
5. Select Zone 1, select AIR FRY, set the temperature to 390°F, and set the time to 35 minutes.
6. Select Zone 2, select BAKE, set the temperature to 340°F, and set the time to 20 minutes. Select SMART FINISH.
7. Press START/PAUSE to begin cooking.
8. When the Zone 2 timer reads 10 minutes, press START/PAUSE. Remove the basket and stir the stuffing. Reinsert the basket and press START/PAUSE to resume cooking.
9. When cooking is complete, the turkey will be cooked through and the stuffing will have absorbed all the liquid and be slightly crisp on top. Serve warm.

Spiced Chicken And Vegetables

Servings:1
Cooking Time:45
Ingredients:

- 2 large chicken breasts
- 2 teaspoons of olive oil
- 1 teaspoon of chili powder
- 1 teaspoon of paprika powder
- 1 teaspoon of onion powder
- ½ teaspoon of garlic powder
- 1/4 teaspoon of Cumin
- Salt and black pepper, to taste
- Vegetable Ingredients:
- 2 large potato, cubed
- 4 large carrots cut into bite-size pieces
- 1 tablespoon of olive oil
- Salt and black pepper, to taste

Directions:

1. Take chicken breast pieces and rub olive oil, salt, pepper, chili powder, onion powder, cumin, garlic powder, and paprika.
2. Season the vegetables with olive oil, salt, and black pepper.
3. Now put the chicken breast pieces in the zone 1 basket.
4. Put the vegetables into the zone 2 basket.
5. Now hit 1 for the first basket and set it to ROAST at 350 degrees F, for 45 minutes.
6. For the second basket hit 2 and set time for 45 minutes, by selecting AIR FRY mode at 350 degrees F.
7. To start cooking hit the smart finish button and press hit start.
8. Once the cooking cycle is done, serve, and enjoy.

Nutrition:

- (Per serving) Calories1510 | Fat 51.3g| Sodium 525mg | Carbs 163g | Fiber24.7 g | Sugar 21.4g | Protein 102.9

Chicken Fajitas With Street Corn

Servings: 4
Cooking Time: 20 Minutes
Ingredients:

- FOR THE FAJITAS
- 1½ pounds boneless, skinless chicken breasts, cut into strips
- 2 bell peppers (red, orange, yellow, or a combination), sliced into ½-inch-wide strips
- 1 small red onion, sliced
- 1 tablespoon vegetable oil
- 2 teaspoons chili powder
- 1 teaspoon ground cumin
- 1 teaspoon kosher salt
- ½ teaspoon freshly ground black pepper
- ½ teaspoon paprika
- ¼ cup fresh cilantro, chopped
- Juice of 1 lime
- 8 (6-inch) flour tortillas
- FOR THE CORN
- ¼ cup mayonnaise
- ¼ cup sour cream
- ¼ cup crumbled Cotija or feta cheese
- 2 tablespoons chopped fresh cilantro
- 1 teaspoon minced garlic
- ½ teaspoon chili powder
- 4 ears corn, husked

Directions:

1. To prep the fajitas: In a large bowl, combine the chicken, bell peppers, onion, oil, chili powder, cumin, salt, black pepper, and paprika and toss to coat.
2. To prep the corn: In a shallow dish, combine the mayonnaise, sour cream, cheese, cilantro, garlic, and chili powder. Mix well and set aside.
3. To cook the fajitas and corn: Install a crisper plate in each of the two baskets. Place the fajita filling in the Zone 1 basket and insert the basket in the unit. Place the corn ears in the Zone 2 basket and insert the basket in the unit.
4. Select Zone 1, select AIR FRY, set the temperature to 390°F, and set the time to 20 minutes.
5. Select Zone 2, select AIR BROIL, set the temperature to 450°F, and set the time to 12 minutes. Select SMART FINISH.
6. Press START/PAUSE to begin cooking.
7. When both timers read 6 minutes, press START/PAUSE. Remove the Zone 1 basket, shake to redistribute the fajita filling, and reinsert the basket. Remove the Zone 2 basket and use silicone-tipped tongs to flip the corn. Reinsert the basket and press START/PAUSE to resume cooking.
8. When cooking is complete, the chicken will be fully cooked and the vegetables will be slightly charred.
9. Mix the cilantro and lime juice into the fajita filling. Divide the filling among the tortillas. Roll the corn in the mayonnaise and cheese mixture to coat. Serve hot.

Chicken Leg Piece

Servings:1
Cooking Time:25
Ingredients:

- 1 teaspoon of onion powder
- 1 teaspoon of paprika powder
- 1 teaspoon of garlic powder
- Salt and black pepper, to taste
- 1 tablespoon of Italian seasoning
- 1 teaspoon of celery seeds
- 2 eggs, whisked
- 1/3 cup buttermilk
- 1 cup of corn flour
- 1 pound of chicken leg

Directions:

1. Take a bowl and whisk egg along with pepper, salt, and buttermilk.
2. Set it aside for further use.
3. Mix all the spices in a small separate bowl.
4. Dredge the chicken in egg wash then dredge it in seasoning.
5. Coat the chicken legs with oil spray.
6. At the end dust it with the corn flour.
7. Divide the leg pieces into two zones.
8. Set zone 1 basket to 400 degrees F, for 25 minutes.
9. Select MATCH for zone 2 basket.
10. Let the air fryer do the magic.
11. Once it's done, serve and enjoy.

Nutrition:

- (Per serving) Calories 1511| Fat 52.3g| Sodium615 mg | Carbs 100g | Fiber 9.2g | Sugar 8.1g | Protein 154.2g

Chicken Wings

Servings:3
Cooking Time:20

Ingredients:

- 1 cup chicken batter mix, Louisiana
- 9 Chicken wings
- ½ teaspoon of smoked paprika
- 2 tablespoons of Dijon mustard
- 1 tablespoon of cayenne pepper
- 1 teaspoon of meat tenderizer, powder
- oil spray, for greasing

Directions:

1. Pat dry chicken wings and add mustard, paprika, meat tenderizer, and cayenne pepper.
2. Dredge it in the chicken batter mix.
3. Oil sprays the chicken wings.
4. Grease both baskets of the air fryer.
5. Divide the wings between the two zones of the air fryer.
6. Set zone 1 to AR FRY mode at 400 degrees F for 20 minutes
7. Select MATCH for zone 2.
8. Hit start to begin with the cooking.
9. Once the cooking cycle complete, serve, and enjoy hot.

Nutrition:

- (Per serving) Calories621 | Fat 32.6g| Sodium 2016mg | Carbs 46.6g | Fiber 1.1g | Sugar 0.2g | Protein 32.1g

Chicken Vegetable Skewers

Servings: 6
Cooking Time: 15 Minutes

Ingredients:

- 900g chicken breasts, cubed
- 1 bell pepper, chopped
- 51g Swerve
- 1 tsp ginger, grated
- 350g zucchini, chopped
- 8 mushrooms, sliced
- ½ medium onion, chopped
- 6 garlic cloves, crushed
- 120ml soy sauce

Directions:

1. Add chicken and the remaining ingredients to a zip-lock bag. Seal the bag and place it in the refrigerator overnight.
2. Thread the marinated chicken, zucchini, mushrooms, onion, and bell pepper onto the skewers.
3. Insert a crisper plate in the Tefal air fryer baskets.
4. Place skewers in both baskets.
5. Select zone 1 then select "air fry" mode and set the temperature to 380 degrees F for 15 minutes. Press "match" to match zone 2 settings to zone 1. Press "start/stop" to begin.

Nutrition:

- (Per serving) Calories 329 | Fat 11.5g |Sodium 1335mg | Carbs 8.6g | Fiber 1.4g | Sugar 2.9g | Protein 46.8g

Cornish Hen With Baked Potatoes

Servings:2
Cooking Time:45

Ingredients:

- Salt, to taste
- 1 large potato
- 1 tablespoon of avocado oil
- 1.5 pounds of Cornish hen, skinless and whole
- 2-3 teaspoons of poultry seasoning, dry rub

Directions:

1. Take a fork and pierce the large potato.
2. Rub the potato with avocado oil and salt.
3. Now put the potatoes in the first basket.
4. Now pick the Cornish hen and season the hen with poultry seasoning (dry rub) and salt.
5. Remember to coat the whole Cornish hen well.
6. Put the potato in zone 1 basket.
7. Now place the hen into zone 2 baskets.
8. Now hit 1 for the first basket and set it to AIR FRY mode at 350 degrees F, for 45 minutes.
9. For the second basket hit 2 and set the time to 45 minutes at 350 degrees F.
10. To start cooking, hit the smart finish button and press hit start.
11. Once the cooking cycle complete, turn off the air fryer and take out the potatoes and Cornish hen from both air fryer baskets.
12. Serve hot and enjoy.

Nutrition:

- (Per serving) Calories 612 | Fat14.3 g| Sodium 304mg | Carbs33.4 g | Fiber 4.5 g | Sugar 1.5g | Protein 83.2 g

Whole Chicken

Servings: 8
Cooking Time: 20 Minutes

Ingredients:

- 1 whole chicken (about 2.8 pounds), cut in half
- 4 tablespoons olive oil
- 2 teaspoons paprika
- 1 teaspoon garlic powder
- 1 teaspoon onion powder
- Salt and pepper, to taste

Directions:

1. Mix the olive oil, paprika, garlic powder, and onion powder together in a bowl.
2. Place the chicken halves, breast side up, on a plate. Spread a teaspoon or two of the oil mix all over the halves using either your hands or a brush. Season with salt and pepper.
3. Flip the chicken halves over and repeat on the other side. You'll want to reserve a little of the oil mix for later, but other than that, use it liberally.
4. Install a crisper plate in both drawers. Place one half of the chicken in the zone 1 drawer and the other half in the zone 2 drawer, then insert the drawers into the unit.
5. Select zone 1, select AIR FRY, set temperature to 390 degrees F/ 200 degrees C, and set time to 20 minutes. Select MATCH to match zone 2 settings to zone 1. Press the START/STOP button to begin cooking.
6. When cooking is done, check the internal temperature of the chicken. It should read 165°F. If the chicken isn't done, add more cooking time.

Nutrition:

- (Per serving) Calories 131 | Fat 8g | Sodium 51mg | Carbs 0g | Fiber 0g | Sugar 0g | Protein 14g

Greek Chicken Souvlaki

Servings: 3 To 4
Cooking Time: 15 Minutes

Ingredients:

- Chicken:
- Grated zest and juice of 1 lemon
- 2 tablespoons extra-virgin olive oil
- 1 tablespoon Greek souvlaki seasoning
- 450 g boneless, skinless chicken breast, cut into 2-inch chunks
- Vegetable oil spray
- For Serving:
- Warm pita bread or hot cooked rice
- Sliced ripe tomatoes
- Sliced cucumbers
- Thinly sliced red onion
- Kalamata olives
- Tzatziki

Directions:

1. For the chicken: In a small bowl, combine the lemon zest, lemon juice, olive oil, and souvlaki seasoning. Place the chicken in a gallon-size resealable plastic bag. Pour the marinade over chicken. Seal bag and massage to coat. Place the bag in a large bowl and marinate for 30 minutes, or cover and refrigerate up to 24 hours, turning the bag occasionally. 2. Place the chicken a single layer in the zone 1 air fryer drawer. Cook at 180°C for 10 minutes, turning the chicken and spraying with a little vegetable oil spray halfway through the cooking time. Increase the air fryer temperature to 200°C for 5 minutes to allow the chicken to crisp and brown a little. 3. Transfer the chicken to a serving platter and serve with pita bread or rice, tomatoes, cucumbers, onion, olives and tzatziki.

Bruschetta Chicken

Servings: 4
Cooking Time: 20 Minutes

Ingredients:

- Bruschetta Stuffing:
- 1 tomato, diced
- 3 tablespoons balsamic vinegar
- 1 teaspoon Italian seasoning
- 2 tablespoons chopped fresh basil
- 3 garlic cloves, minced
- 2 tablespoons extra-virgin olive oil
- Chicken:
- 4 (115 g) boneless, skinless chicken breasts, cut 4 slits each
- 1 teaspoon Italian seasoning
- Chicken seasoning or rub, to taste
- Cooking spray

Directions:

1. Preheat the air fryer to 190°. Spritz the two air fryer baskets with cooking spray.
2. Combine the ingredients for the bruschetta stuffing in a bowl. Stir to mix well. Set aside.
3. Rub the chicken breasts with Italian seasoning and chicken seasoning on a clean work surface.
4. Arrange the chicken breasts, slits side up, in a single layer in the two air fryer baskets and spritz with cooking spray.
5. Air fry for 7 minutes, then open the air fryer and fill the slits in the chicken with the bruschetta stuffing. Cook for another 3 minutes or until the chicken is well browned.
6. Serve immediately.

Crispy Dill Chicken Strips

Servings: 4
Cooking Time: 10 Minutes

Ingredients:

- 2 whole boneless, skinless chicken breasts (about 450 g each), halved lengthwise
- 230 ml Italian dressing
- 110 g finely crushed crisps
- 1 tablespoon dried dill weed
- 1 tablespoon garlic powder
- 1 large egg, beaten
- 1 to 2 tablespoons oil

Directions:

1. In a large resealable bag, combine the chicken and Italian dressing. Seal the bag and refrigerate to marinate at least 1 hour.
2. In a shallow dish, stir together the potato chips, dill, and garlic powder. Place the beaten egg in a second shallow dish.
3. Remove the chicken from the marinade. Roll the chicken pieces in the egg and the crisp mixture, coating thoroughly.
4. Preheat the air fryer to 170°C. Line the two air fryer drawers with parchment paper.
5. Place the coated chicken on the parchment and spritz with oil.
6. Cook for 5 minutes. Flip the chicken, spritz it with oil, and cook for 5 minutes more until the outsides are crispy and the insides are no longer pink.

Crusted Chicken Breast

Servings: 4
Cooking Time: 28 Minutes

Ingredients:

- 2 large eggs, beaten
- ½ cup all-purpose flour
- 1 ¼ cups panko bread crumbs
- ⅔ cup Parmesan, grated
- 4 teaspoons lemon zest
- 2 teaspoons dried oregano
- Salt, to taste
- 1 teaspoon cayenne pepper
- Freshly black pepper, to taste
- 4 boneless skinless chicken breasts

Directions:

1. Beat eggs in one shallow bowl and spread flour in another shallow bowl.
2. Mix panko with oregano, lemon zest, Parmesan, cayenne, oregano, salt, and black pepper in another shallow bowl.
3. First, coat the chicken with flour first, then dip it in the eggs and coat them with panko mixture.
4. Arrange the prepared chicken in the two crisper plates.
5. Return the crisper plate to the Tefal Dual Zone Air Fryer.
6. Choose the Air Fry mode for Zone 1 and set the temperature to 390 degrees F and the time to 28 minutes|
7. Select the "MATCH" button to copy the settings for Zone 2.
8. Initiate cooking by pressing the START/STOP button.
9. Flip the half-cooked chicken and continue cooking for 5 minutes until golden.
10. Serve warm.

Curried Orange Honey Chicken

Servings: 4
Cooking Time: 16 To 19 Minutes

Ingredients:

- 340 g boneless, skinless chicken thighs, cut into 1-inch pieces
- 1 yellow bell pepper, cut into 1½-inch pieces
- 1 small red onion, sliced
- Olive oil for misting
- 60 ml chicken stock
- 2 tablespoons honey
- 60 ml orange juice
- 1 tablespoon cornflour
- 2 to 3 teaspoons curry powder

Directions:

1. Preheat the air fryer to 190°C.
2. Put the chicken thighs, pepper, and red onion in the zone 1 air fryer drawer and mist with olive oil.
3. Roast for 12 to 14 minutes or until the chicken is cooked to 76°C, shaking the drawer halfway through cooking time.
4. Remove the chicken and vegetables from the air fryer drawer and set aside.
5. In a metal bowl, combine the stock, honey, orange juice, cornflour, and curry powder, and mix well. Add the chicken and vegetables, stir, and put the bowl in the drawer.
6. Return the drawer to the air fryer and roast for 2 minutes. Remove and stir, then roast for 2 to 3 minutes or until the sauce is thickened and bubbly.
7. Serve warm.

Beef, Pork, And Lamb Recipes

Cheesy Low-carb Lasagna

Servings: 4
Cooking Time: 10 Minutes

Ingredients:

- Meat Layer:
- Extra-virgin olive oil
- 450 g 85% lean beef mince
- 235 ml marinara sauce
- 60 ml diced celery
- 60 ml diced red onion
- ½ teaspoon minced garlic
- Coarse or flaky salt and black pepper, to taste
- Cheese Layer:
- 230 g ricotta cheese
- 235 ml shredded Mozzarella cheese
- 120 ml grated Parmesan cheese
- 2 large eggs
- 1 teaspoon dried Italian seasoning, crushed
- ½ teaspoon each minced garlic, garlic powder, and black pepper

Directions:

1. For the meat layer: Grease a cake pan with 1 teaspoon olive oil. 2. In a large bowl, combine the beef mince, marinara, celery, onion, garlic, salt, and pepper. Place the seasoned meat in the pan. 3. Place the pan in the zone 1 air fryer drawer. Set the temperature to 192°C for 10 minutes. 4. Meanwhile, for the cheese layer: In a medium bowl, combine the ricotta, half the Mozzarella, the Parmesan, lightly beaten eggs, Italian seasoning, minced garlic, garlic powder, and pepper. Stir until well blended. 5. At the end of the cooking time, spread the cheese mixture over the meat mixture. Sprinkle with the remaining 120 ml Mozzarella. Set the temperature to 192°C for 10 minutes, or until the cheese is browned and bubbling. 6. At the end of the cooking time, use a meat thermometer to ensure the meat has reached an internal temperature of 72°C. 7. Drain the fat and liquid from the pan. Let stand for 5 minutes before serving.

Kielbasa Sausage With Pineapple And Kheema Meatloaf

Servings: 6 To 8
Cooking Time: 15 Minutes

Ingredients:

- Kielbasa Sausage with Pineapple:
- 340 g kielbasa sausage, cut into ½-inch slices
- 1 (230 g) can pineapple chunks in juice, drained
- 235 ml pepper chunks
- 1 tablespoon barbecue seasoning
- 1 tablespoon soy sauce
- Cooking spray
- Kheema Meatloaf:
- 450 g 85% lean beef mince
- 2 large eggs, lightly beaten
- 235 ml diced brown onion
- 60 ml chopped fresh coriander
- 1 tablespoon minced fresh ginger
- 1 tablespoon minced garlic
- 2 teaspoons garam masala
- 1 teaspoon coarse or flaky salt
- 1 teaspoon ground turmeric
- 1 teaspoon cayenne pepper
- ½ teaspoon ground cinnamon
- ⅛ teaspoon ground cardamom

Directions:

1. Make the Kielbasa Sausage with Pineapple :
2. Preheat the air fryer to 200°C. Spritz the zone 1 air fryer drawer with cooking spray.
3. Combine all the ingredients in a large bowl. Toss to mix well.
4. Pour the sausage mixture in the preheated zone 1 air fryer drawer.
5. Air fry for 10 minutes or until the sausage is lightly browned and the pepper and pineapple are soft. Shake the drawer halfway through. Serve immediately.
6. Make the Kheema Meatloaf :
7. In a large bowl, gently mix the beef mince, eggs, onion, coriander, ginger, garlic, garam masala, salt, turmeric, cayenne, cinnamon, and cardamom until thoroughly combined.
8. Place the seasoned meat in a baking pan. Place the pan in the zone 2 air fryer drawer. Set the temperature to 176°C for 15 minutes. Use a meat thermometer to ensure the meat loaf has reached an internal temperature of 72°C .
9. Drain the fat and liquid from the pan and let stand for 5 minutes before slicing.
10. Slice and serve hot.

Steaks With Walnut-blue Cheese Butter

Servings: 6
Cooking Time: 10 Minutes
Ingredients:

- 120 ml unsalted butter, at room temperature
- 120 ml crumbled blue cheese
- 2 tablespoons finely chopped walnuts
- 1 tablespoon minced fresh rosemary
- 1 teaspoon minced garlic
- ¼ teaspoon cayenne pepper
- Sea salt and freshly ground black pepper, to taste
- 680 g sirloin steaks, at room temperature

Directions:

1. In a medium bowl, combine the butter, blue cheese, walnuts, rosemary, garlic, and cayenne pepper and salt and black pepper to taste. Use clean hands to ensure that everything is well combined. Place the mixture on a sheet of parchment paper and form it into a log. Wrap it tightly in plastic wrap. Refrigerate for at least 2 hours or freeze for 30 minutes.
2. Season the steaks generously with salt and pepper.
3. Set the air fryer to 204°C and let it preheat for 5 minutes.
4. Place the steaks in the two drawers in a single layer and air fry for 5 minutes. Flip the steaks, and cook for 5 minutes more, until an instant-read thermometer reads 49°C for medium-rare .
5. Transfer the steaks to a plate. Cut the butter into pieces and place the desired amount on top of the steaks. Tent a piece of aluminum foil over the steaks and allow to sit for 10 minutes before serving.
6. Store any remaining butter in a sealed container in the refrigerator for up to 2 weeks.

Bacon-wrapped Filet Mignon

Servings: 4
Cooking Time: 15 Minutes
Ingredients:

- 4 bacon slices
- 4 (4-ounce) filet mignon
- Salt and ground black pepper, as required
- Olive oil cooking spray

Directions:

1. Wrap 1 bacon slice around each filet mignon and secure with toothpicks.
2. Spray the filet mignon with cooking spray evenly. Season the filets with salt and black pepper lightly.
3. Grease each basket of "Zone 1" and "Zone 2" of Tefal 2-Basket Air Fryer.
4. Press "Zone 1" and "Zone 2" and then rotate the knob for each zone to select "Air Fry".
5. Set the temperature to 400 degrees F/ 200 degrees C for both zones and then set the time for 5 minutes to preheat.
6. After preheating, arrange 2 filets into the basket of each zone.
7. Slide each basket into Air Fryer and set the time for 15 minutes.
8. While cooking, flip the filets once halfway through.
9. After cooking time is completed, remove the filets from Air Fryer and serve hot.

Simple Strip Steak

Servings: 4
Cooking Time: 10 Minutes
Ingredients:

- 2 (9½-ounce) New York strip steaks
- Salt and ground black pepper, as required
- 3 teaspoons olive oil

Directions:

1. Grease each basket of "Zone 1" and "Zone 2" of Tefal 2-Basket Air Fryer.
2. Press "Zone 1" and "Zone 2" and then rotate the knob for each zone to select "Air Fry".
3. Set the temperature to 400 degrees F/ 200 degrees C for both zones and then set the time for 5 minutes to preheat.
4. Coat the steaks with oil and then sprinkle with salt and black pepper evenly.
5. After preheating, arrange 1 steak into the basket of each zone.
6. Slide each basket into Air Fryer and set the time for 10 minutes.
7. While cooking, flip the steak once halfway through.
8. After cooking time is completed, remove the steaks from Air Fryer and place onto a platter for about 10 minutes.
9. Cut each steak into desired size slices and serve immediately.

Bacon-wrapped Hot Dogs With Mayo-ketchup Sauce

Servings: 5
Cooking Time: 10 To 12 Minutes
Ingredients:

- 10 thin slices of bacon
- 5 pork hot dogs, halved
- 1 teaspoon cayenne pepper
- Sauce:
- 60 ml mayonnaise
- 4 tablespoons ketchup
- 1 teaspoon rice vinegar
- 1 teaspoon chili powder

Directions:

1. Preheat the air fryer to 200°C. 2. Arrange the slices of bacon on a clean work surface. One by one, place the halved hot dog on one end of each slice, season with cayenne pepper and wrap the hot dog with the bacon slices and secure with toothpicks as needed. 3. Place half the wrapped hot dogs in the two air fryer drawers and air fry for 10 to 12 minutes or until the bacon becomes browned and crispy. 4. Make the sauce: Stir all the ingredients for the sauce in a small bowl. Wrap the bowl in plastic and set in the refrigerator until ready to serve. 5. Transfer the hot dogs to a platter and serve hot with the sauce.

Spice-rubbed Pork Loin

Servings: 6
Cooking Time: 20 Minutes
Ingredients:

- 1 teaspoon paprika
- ½ teaspoon ground cumin
- ½ teaspoon chili powder
- ½ teaspoon garlic powder
- 2 tablespoons coconut oil
- 1 (680 g) boneless pork loin
- ½ teaspoon salt
- ¼ teaspoon ground black pepper

Directions:

1. In a small bowl, mix paprika, cumin, chili powder, and garlic powder.
2. Drizzle coconut oil over pork. Sprinkle pork loin with salt and pepper, then rub spice mixture evenly on all sides.
3. Place pork loin into the two ungreased air fryer drawer. Adjust the temperature to 204°C and air fry for 20 minutes, turning pork halfway through cooking. Pork loin will be browned and have an internal temperature of at least 64°C when done. Serve warm.

Pigs In A Blanket And Currywurst

Servings: 6
Cooking Time: 12 Minutes
Ingredients:

- Pigs in a Blanket:
- 120 ml shredded Mozzarella cheese
- 2 tablespoons blanched finely ground almond flour
- 30 g full-fat cream cheese
- 2 (110 g) beef smoked sausage, cut in two
- ½ teaspoon sesame seeds
- Currywurst:
- 235 ml tomato sauce
- 2 tablespoons cider vinegar
- 2 teaspoons curry powder
- 2 teaspoons sweet paprika
- 1 teaspoon sugar
- ¼ teaspoon cayenne pepper
- 1 small onion, diced
- 450 g bratwurst, sliced diagonally into 1-inch pieces

Directions:

1. Make the Pigs in a Blanket : Place Mozzarella, almond flour, and cream cheese in a large microwave-safe bowl. Microwave for 45 seconds and stir until smooth. Roll dough into a ball and cut in half. 2. Press each half out into a 4 × 5-inch rectangle. Roll one sausage up in each dough half and press seams closed. Sprinkle the top with sesame seeds. 3. Place each wrapped sausage into the zone 1 air fryer drawer. 4. Adjust the temperature to 204°C and air fry for 7 minutes. 5. The outside will be golden when completely cooked. Serve immediately.
2. Make the Currywurst : 1. In a large bowl, combine the tomato sauce, vinegar, curry powder, paprika, sugar, and cayenne. Whisk until well combined. Stir in the onion and bratwurst. Transfer the mixture to a baking pan. Place the pan in the zone 2 air fryer drawer. Set the temperature to 204°C for 12 minutes, or until the sausage is heated through and the sauce is bubbling.

Beef & Broccoli

Servings:4
Cooking Time:12
Ingredients:

- 12 ounces of teriyaki sauce, divided
- ½ tablespoon garlic powder
- ¼ cup of soy sauce
- 1 pound raw sirloin steak, thinly sliced
- 2 cups broccoli, cut into florets
- 2 teaspoons of olive oil
- Salt and black pepper, to taste

Directions:

1. Take a zip-lock plastic bag and mix teriyaki sauce, salt, garlic powder, black pepper, soy sauce, and olive oil.
2. Marinate the beef in it for 2 hours.
3. Then drain the beef from the marinade.
4. Now toss the broccoli with oil, teriyaki sauce, and salt and black pepper.
5. Put it in a zone 1 basket
6. Now for the zone, 1 basket set it to AIRFRY mode at 400 degrees F for 15 minutes.
7. Place the steak in a zone 2 basket and set it to AIR FRY mode at 375 degrees F for 10-12 minutes.
8. Hit start and let the cooking cycle completes.
9. Once it's done take out the beef and broccoli and
10. serve immediately with leftover teriyaki sauce and cooked rice.

Nutrition:

- (Per serving) Calories 344| Fat 10g| Sodium 4285mg | Carbs18.2 g | Fiber 1.5g| Sugar 13.3g | Protein42 g

Turkey And Beef Meatballs

Servings: 6
Cooking Time: 24 Minutes.
Ingredients:

- 1 medium shallot, minced
- 2 tablespoons olive oil
- 3 garlic cloves, minced
- ¼ cup panko crumbs
- 2 tablespoons whole milk
- ⅔ lb. lean ground beef
- ⅓ lb. bulk turkey sausage
- 1 large egg, lightly beaten
- ¼ cup parsley, chopped
- 1 tablespoon fresh thyme, chopped
- 1 tablespoon fresh rosemary, chopped
- 1 tablespoon Dijon mustard
- ½ teaspoon salt

Directions:

1. Preheat your oven to 400 degrees F. Place a medium non-stick pan over medium-high heat.
2. Add oil and shallot, then sauté for 2 minutes.
3. Toss in the garlic and cook for 1 minute.
4. Remove this pan from the heat.
5. Whisk panko with milk in a large bowl and leave it for 5 minutes.
6. Add cooked shallot mixture and mix well.
7. Stir in egg, parsley, turkey sausage, beef, thyme, rosemary, salt, and mustard.
8. Mix well, then divide the mixture into 1 ½-inch balls.
9. Divide these balls into the two crisper plates and spray them with cooking oil.
10. Return the crisper plates to the Tefal Dual Zone Air Fryer.
11. Choose the Air Fry mode for Zone 1 and set the temperature to 400 degrees F and the time to 21 minutes.
12. Select the "MATCH" button to copy the settings for Zone 2.
13. Initiate cooking by pressing the START/STOP button.
14. Serve warm.

Nutrition:

- (Per serving) Calories 551 | Fat 31g |Sodium 1329mg | Carbs 1.5g | Fiber 0.8g | Sugar 0.4g | Protein 64g

Pork Chops

Servings:2
Cooking Time:17
Ingredients:

- 1 tablespoon of rosemary, chopped
- Salt and black pepper, to taste
- 2 garlic cloves
- 1-inch ginger
- 2 tablespoons of olive oil
- 8 pork chops

Directions:

1. Take a blender and pulse together rosemary, salt, pepper, garlic cloves, ginger, and olive oil.
2. Rub this marinade over pork chops and let it rest for 1 hour.
3. Then divide it amongst air fryer baskets and set it to AIR FRY mode for 17 minutes at 375 degrees F.
4. Once the cooking cycle is done, take out and serve hot.

Nutrition:

- (Per serving) Calories 1154| Fat 93.8g| Sodium 225mg | Carbs 2.1g | Fibero.8 g| Sugar 0g | Protein 72.2g

Asian Glazed Meatballs

Servings: 4 To 6
Cooking Time: 10 Minutes

Ingredients:

- 1 large shallot, finely chopped
- 2 cloves garlic, minced
- 1 tablespoon grated fresh ginger
- 2 teaspoons fresh thyme, finely chopped
- 355 ml brown mushrooms, very finely chopped
- 2 tablespoons soy sauce
- Freshly ground black pepper, to taste
- 450 g beef mince
- 230 g pork mince
- 3 egg yolks
- 235 ml Thai sweet chili sauce (spring roll sauce)
- 60 ml toasted sesame seeds
- 2 spring onions, sliced

Directions:

1. Combine the shallot, garlic, ginger, thyme, mushrooms, soy sauce, freshly ground black pepper, beef and pork mince, and egg yolks in a bowl and mix the ingredients together. Gently shape the mixture into 24 balls, about the size of a golf ball.
2. Preheat the air fryer to 192°C.
3. Air fry the meatballs in the two drawers for 8 minutes, turning the meatballs over halfway through the cooking time. Drizzle some of the Thai sweet chili sauce on top of each meatball and return the drawers to the air fryer, air frying for another 2 minutes. Reserve the remaining Thai sweet chili sauce for serving.
4. As soon as the meatballs are done, sprinkle with toasted sesame seeds and transfer them to a serving platter. Scatter the spring onions around and serve warm.

Garlic Sirloin Steak

Servings: 4
Cooking Time: 10 Minutes

Ingredients:

- 4 sirloin steak
- 30ml olive oil
- 28g steak sauce
- ½ tsp ground coriander
- 1 tsp garlic, minced
- 1 tbsp thyme, chopped
- Pepper
- Salt

Directions:

1. In a bowl, mix steak with thyme, oil, steak sauce, coriander, garlic, pepper, and salt. Cover and set aside for 2 hours.
2. Insert a crisper plate in Tefal air fryer baskets.
3. Place the marinated steaks in both baskets.
4. Select zone 1 then select air fry mode and set the temperature to 360 degrees F for 10 minutes. Press "match" and then "start/stop" to begin.

Bbq Pork Spare Ribs

Servings: 8
Cooking Time: 30 Minutes

Ingredients:

- ½ cup honey, divided
- 1½ cups BBQ sauce
- 4 tablespoons tomato ketchup
- 2 tablespoons Worcestershire sauce
- 2 tablespoons low-sodium soy sauce
- 1 teaspoon garlic powder
- Freshly ground white pepper, as required
- 3½ pounds pork ribs

Directions:

1. In a bowl, mix together 6 tablespoons of honey and the remaining ingredients except pork ribs.
2. Add the pork ribs and coat with the mixture generously.
3. Refrigerate to marinate for about 20 minutes.
4. Grease each basket of "Zone 1" and "Zone 2" of Tefal 2-Basket Air Fryer.
5. Press "Zone 1" and "Zone 2" and then rotate the knob for each zone to select "Air Fry".
6. Set the temperature to 355 degrees F/ 180 degrees C for both zones and then set the time for 5 minutes to preheat.
7. After preheating, arrange the ribs into the basket of each zone.
8. Slide each basket into Air Fryer and set the time for 26 minutes.
9. While cooking, flip the ribs once halfway through.
10. After cooking time is completed, remove the ribs from Air Fryer and place onto serving plates.
11. Drizzle with the remaining honey and serve immediately.

Easy Breaded Pork Chops

Servings: 8
Cooking Time: 20 Minutes
Ingredients:

- 1 egg
- 118ml milk
- 8 pork chops
- 1 packet ranch seasoning
- 238g breadcrumbs
- Pepper
- Salt

Directions:
1. In a small bowl, whisk the egg and milk.
2. In a separate shallow dish, mix breadcrumbs, ranch seasoning, pepper, and salt.
3. Dip each pork chop in the egg mixture, then coat with breadcrumbs.
4. Insert a crisper plate in the Tefal air fryer baskets.
5. Place the coated pork chops in both baskets.
6. Select zone 1, then select air fry mode and set the temperature to 360 degrees F for 12 minutes. Press "match" to match zone 2 settings to zone 1. Press "start/stop" to begin. Turn halfway through.

Lamb Shank With Mushroom Sauce

Servings: 4
Cooking Time: 35 Minutes.
Ingredients:

- 20 mushrooms, chopped
- 2 red bell pepper, chopped
- 2 red onion, chopped
- 1 cup red wine
- 4 leeks, chopped
- 6 tablespoons balsamic vinegar
- 2 teaspoons black pepper
- 2 teaspoons salt
- 3 tablespoons fresh rosemary
- 6 garlic cloves
- 4 lamb shanks
- 3 tablespoons olive oil

Directions:
1. Season the lamb shanks with salt, pepper, rosemary, and 1 teaspoon of olive oil.
2. Set half of the shanks in each of the crisper plate.
3. Return the crisper plate to the Tefal Dual Zone Air Fryer.
4. Choose the Air Fry mode for Zone 1 and set the temperature to 390 degrees F and the time to 25 minutes.
5. Select the "MATCH" button to copy the settings for Zone 2.
6. Initiate cooking by pressing the START/STOP button.
7. Flip the shanks halfway through, and resume cooking.
8. Meanwhile, add and heat the remaining olive oil in a skillet.
9. Add onion and garlic to sauté for 5 minutes.
10. Add in mushrooms and cook for 5 minutes.
11. Add red wine and cook until it is absorbed
12. Stir all the remaining vegetables along with black pepper and salt.
13. Cook until vegetables are al dente.
14. Serve the air fried shanks with sautéed vegetable fry.

Nutrition:

- (Per serving) Calories 352 | Fat 9.1g |Sodium 1294mg | Carbs 3.9g | Fiber 1g | Sugar 1g | Protein 61g

Bacon-wrapped Vegetable Kebabs

Servings: 4
Cooking Time: 10 To 12 Minutes
Ingredients:

- 110 g mushrooms, sliced
- 1 small courgette, sliced
- 12 baby plum tomatoes
- 110 g sliced bacon, halved
- Avocado oil spray
- Sea salt and freshly ground black pepper, to taste

Directions:
1. Stack 3 mushroom slices, 1 courgette slice, and 1 tomato. Wrap a bacon strip around the vegetables and thread them onto a skewer. Repeat with the remaining vegetables and bacon. Spray with oil and sprinkle with salt and pepper.
2. Set the air fryer to 204°C. Place the skewers in the two air fryer drawers in a single layer and air fry for 5 minutes. Flip the skewers and cook for 5 to 7 minutes more, until the bacon is crispy and the vegetables are tender.
3. Serve warm.

Steak And Mashed Creamy Potatoes

Servings:1
Cooking Time:45

Ingredients:

- 2 Russet potatoes, peeled and cubed
- ¼ cup butter, divided
- 1/3 cup heavy cream
- ½ cup shredded cheddar cheese
- Salt and black pepper, to taste
- 1 New York strip steak, about a pound
- 1 teaspoon of olive oil
- Oil spray, for greasing

Directions:

1. Rub the potatoes with salt and a little amount of olive oil about a teaspoon.
2. Next, season the steak with salt and black pepper.
3. Place the russet potatoes in a zone 1 basket.
4. Oil spray the steak from both sides and then place it in the zone 2 basket.
5. Set zone 1 to AIR fry mode for 45 minutes at 390 degrees F.
6. Set the zone 2 basket, at 12 minutes at 375 degrees F.
7. Hot start and Lethe Tefal do its magic.
8. One the cooking cycle completes, take out the steak and potatoes.
9. Mash the potatoes and then add butter, heavy cream, and cheese along with salt and black pepper.
10. Serve the mashed potatoes with steak.
11. Enjoy.

Nutrition:

- (Per serving) Calories1932 | Fat 85.2g| Sodium 3069mg | Carbs 82g | Fiber10.3 g| Sugar 5.3g | Protein 22.5g

Mongolian Beef With Sweet Chili Brussels Sprouts

Servings:4
Cooking Time: 20 Minutes

Ingredients:

- FOR THE MONGOLIAN BEEF
- 1 pound flank steak, cut into thin strips
- 1 tablespoon olive oil
- 2 tablespoons cornstarch
- ½ cup reduced-sodium soy sauce
- ½ cup packed light brown sugar
- 1 tablespoon chili paste (optional)
- 1 tablespoon minced garlic
- 1 tablespoon minced fresh ginger
- 2 scallions, chopped
- FOR THE BRUSSELS SPROUTS
- 1 pound Brussels sprouts, halved lengthwise
- 1 tablespoon olive oil
- ½ cup gochujang sauce
- 2 tablespoons rice vinegar
- 1 tablespoon reduced-sodium soy sauce
- 1 tablespoon light brown sugar
- 1 teaspoon fresh garlic

Directions:

1. To prep the Mongolian beef: In a large bowl, combine the flank steak and olive oil and toss to coat. Add the cornstarch and toss to coat.
2. In a small bowl, whisk together the soy sauce, brown sugar, chili paste (if using), garlic, and ginger. Set the soy sauce mixture aside.
3. To prep the Brussels sprouts: In a large bowl, combine the Brussels sprouts and oil and toss to coat.
4. In a small bowl, whisk together the gochujang sauce, vinegar, soy sauce, brown sugar, and garlic. Set the chili sauce mixture aside.
5. To cook the beef and Brussels sprouts: Install a crisper plate in each of the two baskets. Place the beef in the Zone 1 basket and insert the basket in the unit. Place the Brussels sprouts in the Zone 2 basket and insert the basket in the unit.
6. Select Zone 1, select AIR FRY, set the temperature to 390°F, and set the time to 15 minutes.
7. Select Zone 2, select AIR FRY, set the temperature to 400°F, and set the time to 20 minutes. Select SMART FINISH.
8. Press START/PAUSE to begin cooking.
9. When both timers read 5 minutes, press START/PAUSE. Remove the Zone 1 basket, add the reserved soy sauce mixture and the scallions, and toss with the beef. Reinsert the basket. Remove the Zone 2 basket, add the reserved chili sauce mixture, and toss with the Brussels sprouts. Reinsert the basket and press START/PAUSE to resume cooking.
10. When cooking is complete, the steak should be cooked through and the Brussels sprouts tender and slightly caramelized. Serve warm.

Nutrition:

- (Per serving) Calories: 481; Total fat: 16g; Saturated fat: 4.5g; Carbohydrates: 60g; Fiber: 5g; Protein: 27g; Sodium: 2,044mg

Garlic-rosemary Pork Loin With Scalloped Potatoes And Cauliflower

Servings:6
Cooking Time: 50 Minutes

Ingredients:

- FOR THE PORK LOIN
- 2 pounds pork loin roast
- 2 tablespoons vegetable oil
- 2 teaspoons dried thyme
- 2 teaspoons dried crushed rosemary
- 1 teaspoon minced garlic
- ¾ teaspoon kosher salt
- FOR THE SCALLOPED POTATOES AND CAULIFLOWER
- 1 teaspoon vegetable oil
- ¾ pound Yukon Gold potatoes, peeled and very thinly sliced
- 1½ cups cauliflower florets
- ¼ teaspoon kosher salt
- ¼ teaspoon freshly ground black pepper
- 1 tablespoon very cold unsalted butter, grated
- 3 tablespoons all-purpose flour
- 1 cup whole milk
- 1 cup shredded Gruyère cheese

Directions:

1. To prep the pork loin: Coat the pork with the oil. Season with thyme, rosemary, garlic, and salt.
2. To prep the potatoes and cauliflower: Brush the bottom and sides of the Zone 2 basket with the oil. Add one-third of the potatoes to the bottom of the basket and arrange in a single layer. Top with ½ cup of cauliflower florets. Sprinkle a third of the salt and black pepper on top. Scatter one-third of the butter on top and sprinkle on 1 tablespoon of flour. Repeat this step twice more for a total of three layers.
3. Pour the milk over the layered potatoes and cauliflower; it should just cover the top layer. Top with the Gruyère.
4. To cook the pork and scalloped vegetables: Install a crisper plate in the Zone 1 basket. Place the pork loin in the basket and insert the basket in the unit. Insert the Zone 2 basket in the unit.
5. Select Zone 1, select AIR FRY, set the temperature to 390°F, and set the time to 50 minutes.
6. Select Zone 2, select BAKE, set the temperature to 350°F, and set the time to 45 minutes. Select SMART FINISH.
7. Press START/PAUSE to begin cooking.
8. When cooking is complete, the pork will be cooked through (an instant-read thermometer should read 145°F) and the potatoes and cauliflower will be tender.
9. Let the pork rest for at least 15 minutes before slicing and serving with the scalloped vegetables.

Nutrition:

- (Per serving) Calories: 439; Total fat: 25g; Saturated fat: 10g; Carbohydrates: 17g; Fiber: 1.5g; Protein: 37g; Sodium: 431mg

Tomahawk Steak

Servings: 4
Cooking Time: 12 Minutes

Ingredients:

- 4 tablespoons butter, softened
- 2 cloves garlic, minced
- 2 teaspoons chopped fresh parsley
- 1 teaspoon chopped chives
- 1 teaspoon chopped fresh thyme
- 1 teaspoon chopped fresh rosemary
- 2 (2 pounds each) bone-in ribeye steaks
- Kosher salt, to taste
- Freshly ground black pepper, to taste

Directions:

1. In a small bowl, combine the butter and herbs. Place the mixture in the center of a piece of plastic wrap and roll it into a log. Twist the ends together to keep it tight and refrigerate until hardened, about 20 minutes.
2. Season the steaks on both sides with salt and pepper.
3. Install a crisper plate in both drawers. Place one steak in the zone 1 drawer and one in zone 2's, then insert the drawers into the unit.
4. Select zone 1, select AIR FRY, set temperature to 390 degrees F/ 200 degrees C, and set time to 12 minutes. Select MATCH to match zone 2 settings to zone 1. Press the START/STOP button to begin cooking.
5. When the time reaches 10 minutes, press START/STOP to pause the unit. Remove the drawers and flip the steaks. Add the herb-butter to the tops of the steaks. Re-insert the drawers into the unit and press START/STOP to resume cooking.
6. Serve and enjoy!

Nutrition:

- (Per serving) Calories 338 | Fat 21.2g | Sodium 1503mg | Carbs 5.1g | Fiber 0.3g | Sugar 4.6g | Protein 29.3g

Pork Katsu With Seasoned Rice

Servings:4
Cooking Time: 15 Minutes
Ingredients:

- FOR THE PORK KATSU
- 4 thin-sliced boneless pork chops (4 ounces each)
- 2 tablespoons all-purpose flour
- 2 large eggs
- 1 cup panko bread crumbs
- ¼ teaspoon kosher salt
- ¼ teaspoon freshly ground black pepper
- 1 teaspoon vegetable oil
- 3 tablespoons ketchup
- 3 tablespoons Worcestershire sauce
- 1 tablespoon oyster sauce
- ⅛ teaspoon granulated sugar
- FOR THE RICE
- 2 cups dried instant rice (not microwavable)
- 2½ cups water
- 1 tablespoon sesame oil
- 1 teaspoon soy sauce
- 1 tablespoon toasted sesame seeds
- 3 scallions, sliced

Directions:

1. To prep the pork katsu: Place the pork chops between two slices of plastic wrap. Using a meat mallet or rolling pin, pound the pork into ½-inch-thick cutlets.
2. Set up a breading station with three small shallow bowls. Place the flour in the first bowl. In the second bowl, whisk the eggs. Combine the panko, salt, and black pepper in the third bowl.
3. Bread the cutlets in this order: First, dip them in the flour, coating both sides. Then, dip them into the beaten egg. Finally, coat them in panko, gently pressing the bread crumbs to adhere to the pork. Drizzle both sides of the cutlets with the oil.
4. To prep the rice: In the Zone 2 basket, combine the rice, water, sesame oil, and soy sauce. Stir well to ensure all of the rice is submerged in the liquid.
5. To cook the pork and rice: Install a crisper plate in the Zone 1 basket. Place the pork in the basket and insert the basket in the unit. Insert the Zone 2 basket in the unit.
6. Select Zone 1, select AIR FRY, set the temperature to 390°F, and set the time to 15 minutes.
7. Select Zone 2, select BAKE, set the temperature to 350°F, and set the time to 10 minutes. Select SMART FINISH.
8. Press START/PAUSE to begin cooking.
9. When the Zone 1 timer reads 10 minutes, press START/PAUSE. Remove the basket and use silicone-tipped tongs to flip the pork. Reinsert the basket and press START/PAUSE to resume cooking.
10. When cooking is complete, the pork should be crisp and cooked through and the rice tender.
11. Stir the sesame seeds and scallions into the rice. For the sauce to go with the pork, in a small bowl, whisk together the ketchup, Worcestershire sauce, oyster sauce, and sugar. Drizzle the sauce over the pork and serve with the hot rice.

Nutrition:

- (Per serving) Calories: 563; Total fat: 20g; Saturated fat: 5.5g; Carbohydrates: 62g; Fiber: 1g; Protein: 34g; Sodium: 665mg

Cheesesteak Taquitos

Servings: 8
Cooking Time: 12 Minutes
Ingredients:

- 1 pack soft corn tortillas
- 136g beef steak strips
- 2 green peppers, sliced
- 1 white onion, chopped
- 1 pkg dry Italian dressing mix
- 10 slices Provolone cheese
- Cooking spray or olive oil

Directions:

1. Mix beef with cooking oil, peppers, onion, and dressing mix in a bowl.
2. Divide the strips in the air fryer baskets.
3. Return the air fryer basket 1 to Zone 1, and basket 2 to Zone 2 of the Tefal 2-Basket Air Fryer.
4. Choose the "Air Fry" mode for Zone 1 at 375 degrees F and 12 minutes of cooking time.
5. Select the "MATCH COOK" option to copy the settings for Zone 2.
6. Initiate cooking by pressing the START/PAUSE BUTTON.
7. Flip the strips once cooked halfway through.
8. Divide the beef strips in the tortillas and top the beef with a beef slice.
9. Roll the tortillas and serve.

Sausage-stuffed Peppers

Servings: 6

Cooking Time: 28 To 30 Minutes

Ingredients:

- Avocado oil spray
- 230 g Italian-seasoned sausage, casings removed
- 120 ml chopped mushrooms
- 60 ml diced onion
- 1 teaspoon Italian seasoning
- Sea salt and freshly ground black pepper, to taste
- 235 ml keto-friendly marinara sauce
- 3 peppers, halved and seeded
- 85 g low-moisture Mozzarella or other melting cheese, shredded

Directions:

1. Spray a large skillet with oil and place it over medium-high heat. Add the sausage and cook for 5 minutes, breaking up the meat with a wooden spoon. Add the mushrooms, onion, and Italian seasoning, and season with salt and pepper. Cook for 5 minutes more. Stir in the marinara sauce and cook until heated through.
2. Scoop the sausage filling into the pepper halves.
3. Set the air fryer to 176°C. Arrange the peppers in a single layer in the two air fryer drawers. Air fry for 15 minutes.
4. Top the stuffed peppers with the cheese and air fry for 3 to 5 minutes more, until the cheese is melted and the peppers are tender.

Simple Lamb Meatballs

Servings: 4

Cooking Time: 15 Minutes

Ingredients:

- 1-pound ground lamb
- 1 teaspoon ground cinnamon
- 1 teaspoon ground cumin
- 2 teaspoons granulated onion
- 2 tablespoons fresh parsley
- Salt and black pepper, to taste

Directions:

1. Add ground lamb, onion, cinnamon, cumin, parsley, salt and pepper in a large bowl. Mix until well combined.
2. Make 1-inch balls from the mixture and set aside.
3. Grease each basket of "Zone 1" and "Zone 2" of Tefal 2-Basket Air Fryer.
4. Press "Zone 1" and "Zone 2" and then rotate the knob for each zone to select "Air Fry".
5. Set the temperature to 380 degrees F/ 195 degrees C for both zones and then set the time for 5 minutes to preheat.
6. After preheating, arrange the meatballs into the basket of each zone.
7. Slide each basket into Air Fryer and set the time for 12 minutes.
8. Flip the meatballs once halfway through.
9. Take out and serve warm.

Asian Pork Skewers

Servings: 4

Cooking Time: 30 Minutes

Ingredients:

- 450g pork shoulder, sliced
- 30g ginger, peeled and crushed
- ½ tablespoon crushed garlic
- 67½ml soy sauce
- 22½ml honey
- 22½ml rice vinegar
- 10ml toasted sesame oil
- 8 skewers

Directions:

1. Pound the pork slices with a mallet.
2. Mix ginger, garlic, soy sauce, honey, rice vinegar, and sesame oil in a bowl.
3. Add pork slices to the marinade and mix well to coat.
4. Cover and marinate the pork for 30 minutes.
5. Thread the pork on the wooden skewers and place them in the air fryer baskets.
6. Return the air fryer basket 1 to Zone 1, and basket 2 to Zone 2 of the Tefal 2-Basket Air Fryer.
7. Choose the "Air Fry" mode for Zone 1 and set the temperature to 350 degrees F and 25 minutes of cooking time.
8. Select the "MATCH COOK" option to copy the settings for Zone 2.
9. Initiate cooking by pressing the START/PAUSE BUTTON.
10. Flip the skewers once cooked halfway through.
11. Serve warm.

Blue Cheese Steak Salad

Servings: 4
Cooking Time: 22 Minutes

Ingredients:

- 2 tablespoons balsamic vinegar
- 2 tablespoons red wine vinegar
- 1 tablespoon Dijon mustard
- 1 tablespoon granulated sweetener
- 1 teaspoon minced garlic
- Sea salt and freshly ground black pepper, to taste
- 180 ml extra-virgin olive oil
- 450 g boneless rump steak
- Avocado oil spray
- 1 small red onion, cut into 1/4-inch-thick rounds
- 170 g baby spinach
- 120 ml cherry tomatoes, halved
- 85 g blue cheese, crumbled

Directions:

1. In a blender, combine the balsamic vinegar, red wine vinegar, Dijon mustard, sweetener, and garlic. Season with salt and pepper and process until smooth. With the blender running, drizzle in the olive oil. Process until well combined. Transfer to a jar with a tight-fitting lid, and refrigerate until ready to serve .
2. Season the steak with salt and pepper and let sit at room temperature for at least 45 minutes, time permitting.
3. Set the zone 1 air fryer drawer to 204°C. Spray the steak with oil and place it in the zone 1 air fryer drawer. Spray the onion slices with oil and place them in the zone 2 air fryer drawer.
4. In zone 1, air fry for 6 minutes. Flip the steak and spray it with more oil. Air fry for 6 minutes more for medium-rare or until the steak is done to your liking.
5. In zone 2, cook at 204°C for 5 minutes. Flip the onion slices and spray them with more oil. Air fry for 5 minutes more.
6. Transfer the steak to a plate, tent with a piece of aluminum foil, and allow it to rest. Slice the steak diagonally into thin strips. Place the spinach, cherry tomatoes, onion slices, and steak in a large bowl. Toss with the desired amount of dressing. Sprinkle with crumbled blue cheese and serve.

Honey Glazed Bbq Pork Ribs

Servings: 4
Cooking Time: 30 Minutes

Ingredients:

- 2 pounds pork ribs
- 1/4 cup honey, divided
- 1 cup BBQ sauce
- 1/2 teaspoon garlic powder
- 2 tablespoons tomato ketchup
- 1 tablespoon Worcestershire sauce
- 1 tablespoon low-sodium soy sauce
- Freshly ground white pepper, as required

Directions:

1. In a bowl, mix together honey and the remaining ingredients except pork ribs.
2. Add the pork ribs and coat with the mixture generously.
3. Refrigerate to marinate for about 20 minutes.
4. Grease each basket of "Zone 1" and "Zone 2" of Tefal 2-Basket Air Fryer.
5. Press "Zone 1" and "Zone 2" and then rotate the knob for each zone to select "Air Fry".
6. Set the temperature to 355 degrees F/ 180 degrees C for both zones and then set the time for 5 minutes to preheat.
7. After preheating, arrange the ribs into the basket of each zone.
8. Slide each basket into Air Fryer and set the time for 26 minutes.
9. While cooking, flip the ribs once halfway through.
10. After cooking time is completed, remove the ribs from Air Fryer and place onto serving plates.
11. Drizzle with the remaining honey and serve immediately.

Italian Sausage And Cheese Meatballs

Servings: 4
Cooking Time: 20 Minutes

Ingredients:

- 230 g sausage meat with Italian seasoning added to taste
- 230 g 85% lean beef mince
- 120 ml shredded sharp Cheddar cheese
- 1/2 teaspoon onion granules
- 1/2 teaspoon garlic powder
- 1/2 teaspoon black pepper

Directions:

1. In a large bowl, gently mix the sausage meat, beef mince, cheese, onion granules, garlic powder, and pepper until well combined.
2. Form the mixture into 16 meatballs. Place the meatballs in a single layer in the two air fryer drawers. Set the air fryer to 176°C for 20 minutes, turning the meatballs halfway through the cooking time. Use a meat thermometer to ensure the meatballs have reached an internal temperature of 72°C .

Roast Souvlaki-style Pork With Lemon-feta Baby Potatoes

Servings:4

Cooking Time: 40 Minutes

Ingredients:

- FOR THE PORK
- 1½ pounds pork tenderloin, cut into bite-size cubes
- ¼ cup olive oil
- ¼ cup fresh lemon juice
- 2 teaspoons minced garlic
- 2 teaspoons honey
- 1½ teaspoons dried oregano
- ¼ teaspoon kosher salt
- ¼ teaspoon freshly ground black pepper
- FOR THE POTATOES
- 1 pound baby red or yellow potatoes, halved
- 1 tablespoon olive oil
- Grated zest and juice of 1 lemon
- ½ teaspoon kosher salt
- ¼ teaspoon freshly ground black pepper
- ⅓ cup crumbled feta cheese
- 2 tablespoons chopped fresh parsley

Directions:

1. To prep the pork: In a large bowl, combine the pork, oil, lemon juice, garlic, honey, oregano, salt, and black pepper. If desired, cover and refrigerate up to 24 hours.
2. To prep the potatoes: In a large bowl, combine the potatoes, oil, lemon zest, lemon juice, salt, and black pepper. Mix to coat the potatoes.
3. To cook the pork and potatoes: Install a crisper plate in each of the two baskets. Place the pork in the Zone 1 basket and insert the basket in the unit. Place the potatoes in the Zone 2 basket and insert the basket in the unit.
4. Select Zone 1, select ROAST, set the temperature to 390°F, and set the time to 20 minutes.
5. Select Zone 2, select AIR FRY, set the temperature to 400°F, and set the time to 40 minutes. Select SMART FINISH.
6. Press START/PAUSE to begin cooking.
7. When cooking is complete, the pork will be cooked through (an instant-read thermometer should read 145°F) and the potatoes will be tender and beginning to brown around the edges.
8. Stir the feta and parsley into the potatoes. Serve the pork and potatoes while hot.

Nutrition:

- (Per serving) Calories: 395; Total fat: 17g; Saturated fat: 4.5g; Carbohydrates: 24g; Fiber: 2g; Protein: 37g; Sodium: 399mg

Desserts Recipes

Healthy Semolina Pudding

Servings: 4

Cooking Time: 20 Minutes

Ingredients:

- 45g semolina
- 1 tsp vanilla
- 500ml milk
- 115g caster sugar

Directions:

1. Mix semolina and ½ cup milk in a bowl. Slowly add the remaining milk, sugar, and vanilla and mix well.
2. Pour the mixture into four greased ramekins.
3. Insert a crisper plate in the Tefal air fryer baskets.
4. Place ramekins in both baskets.
5. Select zone 1, then select "air fry" mode and set the temperature to 300 degrees F for 20 minutes. Press "match" to match zone 2 settings to zone 1. Press "start/stop" to begin.

Nutrition:

- (Per serving) Calories 209 | Fat 2.7g |Sodium 58mg | Carbs 41.5g | Fiber 0.6g | Sugar 30.6g | Protein 5.8g

Glazed Cherry Turnovers

Servings: 8
Cooking Time: 14 Minutes
Ingredients:

- 2 sheets frozen puff pastry, thawed
- 600 g can premium cherry pie filling
- 2 teaspoons ground cinnamon
- 1 egg, beaten
- 90 g sliced almonds
- 120 g icing sugar
- 2 tablespoons milk

Directions:

1. Roll a sheet of puff pastry out into a square that is approximately 10-inches by 10-inches. Cut this large square into quarters.
2. Mix the cherry pie filling and cinnamon together in a bowl. Spoon ¼ cup of the cherry filling into the center of each puff pastry square. Brush the perimeter of the pastry square with the egg wash. Fold one corner of the puff pastry over the cherry pie filling towards the opposite corner, forming a triangle. Seal the two edges of the pastry together with the tip of a fork, making a design with the tines. Brush the top of the turnovers with the egg wash and sprinkle sliced almonds over each one. Repeat these steps with the second sheet of puff pastry. You should have eight turnovers at the end.
3. Preheat the air fryer to 188°C.
4. Air fry turnovers in the two drawers for 14 minutes, carefully turning them over halfway through the cooking time.
5. While the turnovers are cooking, make the glaze by whisking the icing sugar and milk together in a small bowl until smooth. Let the glaze sit for a minute so the sugar can absorb the milk. If the consistency is still too thick to drizzle, add a little more milk, a drop at a time, and stir until smooth.
6. Let the cooked cherry turnovers sit for at least 10 minutes. Then drizzle the glaze over each turnover in a zigzag motion. Serve warm or at room temperature.

Citrus Mousse

Servings: 4
Cooking Time: 12 Minutes
Ingredients:

- 8 ounces cream cheese, softened
- 1 cup heavy cream
- 4 tablespoons fresh lime juice
- 4 tablespoons maple syrup
- Pinch of salt

Directions:

1. For mousse: Press "Zone 1" and "Zone 2" and then rotate the knob for each zone to select "Bake".
2. Set the temperature to 350 degrees F/ 175 degrees C for both zones and then set the time for 5 minutes to preheat.
3. In a bowl, add all the ingredients and mix until well combined.
4. Transfer the mixture into 4 ramekins.
5. After preheating, arrange 2 ramekins into the basket of each zone.
6. Slide each basket into Air Fryer and set the time for 12 minutes.
7. After cooking time is completed, remove the ramekins from Air Fryer.
8. Set the ramekins aside to cool.
9. Refrigerate the ramekins for at least 3 hours before serving.

Mini Strawberry And Cream Pies

Servings: 2
Cooking Time: 15 Minutes
Ingredients:

- 1 box store-bought pie dough, Trader Joe's
- 1 cup strawberries, cubed
- 3 tablespoons cream, heavy
- 2 tablespoons almonds
- 1 egg white, for brushing

Directions:

1. Take the store-bought pie dough and flatten it on a surface.
2. Use a round cutter to cut it into 3-inch circles.
3. Brush the dough with egg white all around the edges.
4. Now add almonds, strawberries, and cream in a tiny amount in the center of the dough, and top it with another dough circle.
5. Press the edges with a fork to seal it.
6. Make a slit in the middle of the pie and divide them into the baskets.
7. Set zone 1 to AIR FRY mode 360 degrees F for 10 minutes.
8. Select MATCH for zone 2 basket.
9. Once done, serve.

Mocha Pudding Cake Vanilla Pudding Cake

Servings:8

Cooking Time: 25 Minutes

Ingredients:

- FOR THE MOCHA PUDDING CAKE
- 1 cup all-purpose flour
- ⅔ cup granulated sugar
- 1 cup packed light brown sugar, divided
- 5 tablespoons unsweetened cocoa powder, divided
- 2 teaspoons baking powder
- ¼ teaspoon kosher salt
- ½ cup unsweetened almond milk
- 2 teaspoons vanilla extract
- 2 tablespoons vegetable oil
- 1 cup freshly brewed coffee
- FOR THE VANILLA PUDDING CAKE
- 1 cup all-purpose flour
- ⅔ cup granulated sugar, plus ½ cup
- 2 teaspoons baking powder
- ¼ teaspoon kosher salt
- ½ cup unsweetened almond milk
- 2½ teaspoons vanilla extract, divided
- 2 tablespoons vegetable oil
- ¾ cup hot water
- 2 teaspoons cornstarch

Directions:

1. To prep the mocha pudding cake: In a medium bowl, combine the flour, granulated sugar, ½ cup of brown sugar, 3 tablespoons of cocoa powder, the baking powder, and salt. Stir in the almond milk, vanilla, and oil to form a thick batter.
2. Spread the batter in the bottom of the Zone 1 basket. Sprinkle the remaining ½ cup brown sugar and 2 tablespoons of cocoa powder in an even layer over the batter. Gently pour the hot coffee over the batter (do not mix).
3. To prep the vanilla pudding cake: In a medium bowl, combine the flour, ⅔ cup of granulated sugar, the baking powder, and salt. Stir in the almond milk, 2 teaspoons of vanilla, and the oil to form a thick batter.
4. Spread the batter in the bottom of the Zone 2 basket.
5. In a small bowl, whisk together the hot water, cornstarch, and remaining ½ cup of sugar and ½ teaspoon of vanilla. Gently pour over the batter (do not mix).
6. To cook both pudding cakes: Insert both baskets in the unit.
7. Select Zone 1, select BAKE, set the temperature to 330°F, and set the timer to 25 minutes. Select MATCH COOK to match Zone 2 settings to Zone 1.
8. Press START/PAUSE to begin cooking.
9. When cooking is complete, the tops of the cakes should be dry and set.
10. Let the cakes rest for 10 minutes before serving. The pudding will thicken as it cools.

Nutrition:

- (Per serving) Calories: 531; Total fat: 8g; Saturated fat: 1g; Carbohydrates: 115g; Fiber: 3.5g; Protein: 5g; Sodium: 111mg

Gluten-free Spice Cookies

Servings: 4

Cooking Time: 12 Minutes

Ingredients:

- 4 tablespoons unsalted butter, at room temperature
- 2 tablespoons agave nectar
- 1 large egg
- 2 tablespoons water
- 240 g almond flour
- 100 g granulated sugar
- 2 teaspoons ground ginger
- 1 teaspoon ground cinnamon
- ½ teaspoon freshly grated nutmeg
- 1 teaspoon baking soda
- ¼ teaspoon kosher, or coarse sea salt

Directions:

1. Line the bottom of the air fryer basket with baking paper cut to fit.
2. In a large bowl, using a hand mixer, beat together the butter, agave, egg, and water on medium speed until light and fluffy.
3. Add the almond flour, sugar, ginger, cinnamon, nutmeg, baking soda, and salt. Beat on low speed until well combined.
4. Roll the dough into 2-tablespoon balls and arrange them on the baking paper in the basket. Set the air fryer to 165°C, and cook for 12 minutes, or until the tops of cookies are lightly browned.
5. Transfer to a wire rack and let cool completely. Store in an airtight container for up to a week.

Quick Pumpkin Spice Pecans

Servings: 4
Cooking Time: 6 Minutes

Ingredients:

- 1 cup whole pecans
- ¼ cup granular erythritol
- 1 large egg white
- ½ teaspoon ground cinnamon
- ½ teaspoon pumpkin pie spice
- ½ teaspoon vanilla extract

Directions:

1. In a large bowl, mix all ingredients well until pecans are coated evenly. Put into the air fryer basket.
2. Set the temperature to 300°F, then set the timer for 6 minutes.
3. Shake 2-3 times during cooking time.
4. Let it cool completely. Keep in an airtight container up to 3 days.

Chocolate Chip Muffins

Servings: 2
Cooking Time: 15 Minutes

Ingredients:

- Salt, pinch
- 2 eggs
- ⅓ cup brown sugar
- ⅓ cup butter
- 4 tablespoons milk
- ¼ teaspoon vanilla extract
- ½ teaspoon baking powder
- 1 cup all-purpose flour
- 1 pouch chocolate chips, 35 grams

Directions:

1. Take 4 oven-safe ramekins that are the size of a cup and layer them with muffin papers.
2. In a bowl, with an electric beater mix the eggs, brown sugar, butter, milk, and vanilla extract.
3. In another bowl, mix the flour, baking powder, and salt.
4. Mix the dry into the wet slowly.
5. Fold in the chocolate chips and mix them in well.
6. Divide this batter into 4 ramekins and place them into both the baskets.
7. Set the time for zone 1 to 15 minutes at 350 degrees F on AIR FRY mode.
8. Select the MATCH button for the zone 2 basket.
9. If they are not completely done after 15 minutes, AIR FRY for another minute.
10. Once it is done, serve.

Spiced Apple Cake

Servings: 6
Cooking Time: 30 Minutes

Ingredients:

- Vegetable oil
- 2 diced & peeled Gala apples
- 1 tablespoon fresh lemon juice
- 55 g unsalted butter, softened
- 65 g granulated sugar
- 2 large eggs
- 155 g plain flour
- 1½ teaspoons baking powder
- 1 tablespoon apple pie spice
- ½ teaspoon ground ginger
- ¼ teaspoon ground cardamom
- ¼ teaspoon ground nutmeg
- ½ teaspoon kosher, or coarse sea salt
- 60 ml whole milk
- Icing sugar, for dusting

Directions:

1. Grease a 0.7-liter Bundt, or tube pan with oil; set aside.
2. In a medium bowl, toss the apples with the lemon juice until well coated; set aside.
3. In a large bowl, combine the butter and sugar. Beat with an electric hand mixer on medium speed until the sugar has dissolved. Add the eggs and beat until fluffy. Add the flour, baking powder, apple pie spice, ginger, cardamom, nutmeg, salt, and milk. Mix until the batter is thick but pourable.
4. Pour the batter into the prepared pan. Top batter evenly with the apple mixture. Place the pan in the zone 1 air fryer drawer. Set the temperature to 176°C and cook for 30 minutes, or until a toothpick inserted in the center of the cake comes out clean. Close the air fryer and let the cake rest for 10 minutes. Turn the cake out onto a wire rack and cool completely.
5. Right before serving, dust the cake with icing sugar.

Fried Dough With Roasted Strawberries

Servings:4
Cooking Time: 20 Minutes

Ingredients:

- FOR THE FRIED DOUGH
- 6 ounces refrigerated pizza dough, at room temperature
- 2 tablespoons all-purpose flour, for dusting
- 4 tablespoons vegetable oil
- 2 tablespoons powdered sugar
- FOR THE ROASTED STRAWBERRIES
- 2 cups frozen whole strawberries
- 2 tablespoons granulated sugar

Directions:

1. To prep the fried dough: Divide the dough into four equal portions.
2. Dust a clean work surface with the flour. Place one dough portion on the surface and use a rolling pin to roll to a 1/8-inch thickness. Rub both sides of the dough with 1 tablespoon of oil. Repeat with remaining dough portions and oil.
3. To prep the strawberries: Place the strawberries in the Zone 2 basket. Sprinkle the granulated sugar on top.
4. To cook the fried dough and strawberries: Install a crisper plate in the Zone 1 basket. Place 2 dough portions in the basket and insert the basket in the unit. Insert the Zone 2 basket in the unit.
5. Select Zone 1, select AIR FRY, set the temperature to 400°F, and set the timer to 18 minutes.
6. Select Zone 2, select ROAST, set the temperature to 330°F, and set the timer to 20 minutes. Select SMART FINISH.
7. Press START/PAUSE to begin cooking.
8. When both timers read 8 minutes, press START/PAUSE. Remove the Zone 1 basket and transfer the fried dough to a cutting board. Place the 2 remaining dough portions in the basket, then reinsert the basket. Remove the Zone 2 basket and stir the strawberries. Reinsert the basket and press START/PAUSE to resume cooking.
9. When cooking is complete, the dough should be cooked through and the strawberries soft and jammy.
10. Sprinkle the fried dough with powdered sugar. Gently mash the strawberries with a fork. Spoon the strawberries onto each fried dough portion and serve.

Nutrition:

- (Per serving) Calories: 304; Total fat: 15g; Saturated fat: 2.5g; Carbohydrates: 38g; Fiber: 0.5g; Protein: 3g; Sodium: 421mg

Strawberry Nutella Hand Pies

Servings: 8
Cooking Time: 15 Minutes

Ingredients:

- 1 tube pie crust dough
- 3–4 strawberries, finely chopped
- Nutella
- Sugar
- Coconut oil cooking spray

Directions:

1. Roll out the pie dough and place it on a baking sheet. Cut out hearts using a 3-inch heart-shaped cookie cutter as precisely as possible.
2. Gather the leftover dough into a ball and roll it out thinly to make a few more heart shapes. For 8 hand pies, I was able to get 16 hearts from one tube of pie crust.
3. Set aside a baking tray lined with parchment paper.
4. Spread a dollop of Nutella on one of the hearts. Add a few strawberry pieces to the mix. Add a pinch of sugar to the top.
5. Place another heart on top and use a fork to tightly crimp the edges. Gently poke holes in the top of the pie with a fork. Place on a baking sheet. Repeat for all the pies.
6. All of the pies on the tray should be sprayed with coconut oil.
7. Install a crisper plate in both drawers. Place half the pies in the zone 1 drawer and half in zone 2's, then insert the drawers into the unit.
8. Select zone 1, select BAKE, set temperature to 390°F, and set time to 10 minutes. Select MATCH to match zone 2 settings to zone 1. Press the START/STOP button to begin cooking.

Lemony Sweet Twists

Servings: 2
Cooking Time: 10 Minutes
Ingredients:

- 1 box store-bought puff pastry
- ½ teaspoon lemon zest
- 1 tablespoon lemon juice
- 2 teaspoons brown sugar
- Salt, pinch
- 2 tablespoons Parmesan cheese, freshly grated

Directions:

1. Put the puff pastry dough on a clean work surface.
2. In a bowl, combine Parmesan cheese, brown sugar, salt, lemon zest, and lemon juice.
3. Press this mixture into both sides of the dough.
4. Now, cut the pastry into 1" x 4" strips.
5. Twist 2 times from each end.
6. Place the strips into the air fryer baskets.
7. Select zone 1 to AIR FRY mode at 400 degrees F for 9-10 minutes.
8. Select MATCH for zone 2 basket.
9. Once cooked, serve and enjoy.

Peanut Butter, Honey & Banana Toast

Servings: 4
Cooking Time: 9 Minutes
Ingredients:

- 2 tablespoons unsalted butter, softened
- 4 slices white bread
- 4 tablespoons peanut butter
- 2 bananas, peeled and thinly sliced
- 4 tablespoons honey
- 1 teaspoon ground cinnamon

Directions:

1. Spread butter on one side of each slice of bread, then peanut butter on the other side. Arrange the banana slices on top of the peanut butter sides of each slice . Drizzle honey on top of the banana and sprinkle with cinnamon.
2. Cut each slice in half lengthwise so that it will better fit into the air fryer basket. Arrange the bread slices, butter sides down, in the two air fryer baskets. Set the air fryer to 190°C cooking for 5 minutes. Then set the air fryer to 205°C and cook for an additional 4 minutes, or until the bananas have started to brown. Serve hot.

Delicious Apple Fritters

Servings: 10
Cooking Time: 8 Minutes
Ingredients:

- 236g Bisquick
- 2 apples, peel & dice
- 158ml milk
- 30ml butter, melted
- 1 tsp cinnamon
- 24g sugar

Directions:

1. In a bowl, mix Bisquick, cinnamon, and sugar.
2. Add milk and mix until dough forms. Add apple and stir well.
3. Insert a crisper plate in Tefal air fryer baskets.
4. Make fritters from the mixture and place in both baskets. Brush fritters with melted butter.
5. Select zone 1 then select "air fry" mode and set the temperature to 360 degrees F for 10 minutes. Press "match" to match zone 2 settings to zone 1. Press "start/stop" to begin.

Nutrition:

- (Per serving) Calories 171 | Fat 6.7g |Sodium 352mg | Carbs 25.8g | Fiber 1.7g | Sugar 10.8g | Protein 2.7g

Quickie Cinnamon Sugar Pork Rinds

Servings: 2
Cooking Time: 5 Minutes
Ingredients:

- 2 ounces pork rinds
- 2 tablespoons unsalted butter, melted
- ½ teaspoon ground cinnamon
- ¼ cup powdered erythritol

Directions:

1. Stir butter and pork rinds in a large bowl. Sprinkle with erythritol and cinnamon, then toss to coat well.
2. Put pork rinds into the air fryer basket.
3. Set the temperature to 400°F, then set the timer for 5 minutes.
4. Serve warm.

Fried Cheesecake Bites

Servings: 16 Bites

Cooking Time: 2 Minutes

Ingredients:

- 225 g cream cheese, softened
- 50 g powdered sweetener, plus 2 tablespoons, divided
- 4 tablespoons heavy cream, divided
- ½ teaspoon vanilla extract
- 50 g almond flour

Directions:

1. In a stand mixer fitted with a paddle attachment, beat the cream cheese, 50 g of the sweetener, 2 tablespoons of the heavy cream, and the vanilla until smooth. Using a small ice-cream scoop, divide the mixture into 16 balls and arrange them on a rimmed baking sheet lined with baking paper. Freeze for 45 minutes until firm.
2. Line the two air fryer drawers with baking paper and preheat the air fryer to 176°C.
3. In a small shallow bowl, combine the almond flour with the remaining 2 tablespoons of sweetener.
4. In another small shallow bowl, place the remaining 2 tablespoons cream.
5. One at a time, dip the frozen cheesecake balls into the cream and then roll in the almond flour mixture, pressing lightly to form an even coating. Arrange the balls in a single layer in the two air fryer drawers, leaving room between them. Air fry for 2 minutes until the coating is lightly browned.

Cake In The Air Fryer

Servings:2

Cooking Time:30

Ingredients:

- 90 grams all-purpose flour
- Pinch of salt
- 1/2 teaspoon of baking powder
- ½ cup of tutti fruitti mix
- 2 eggs
- 1 teaspoon of vanilla extract
- 10 tablespoons of white sugar

Directions:

1. Take a bowl and add all-purpose flour, salt, and baking powder.
2. Stir it in a large bowl.
3. Whisk two eggs in a separate bowl and add vanilla extract, sugar and blend it with a hand beater.
4. Now combine wet ingredients with the dry ones.
5. Mix it well and pour it between two round pan that fits inside baskets.
6. Place the pans in both the baskets.
7. Now set the zone 1 basket to BAKE function at 310 for 30 minutes.
8. Select MATCH for zone two baskets.
9. Once it's done, serve and enjoy.

Nutrition:

- (Per serving) Calories 711| Fat4.8g| Sodium 143mg | Carbs 161g | Fiber 1.3g | Sugar 105g | Protein 10.2g

Baked Apples

Servings: 4

Cooking Time: 20 Minutes

Ingredients:

- 4 granny smith apples, halved and cored
- ¼ cup old-fashioned oats (not the instant kind)
- 1 tablespoon butter, melted
- 2 tablespoon brown sugar
- ½ teaspoon ground cinnamon
- Whipped cream, for topping (optional)

Directions:

1. Insert the crisper plates into the drawers. Lay the cored apple halves in a single layer into each of the drawers . Insert the drawers into the unit.
2. Select zone 1, select AIR FRY, set temperature to 350°F, and set time to 10 minutes. Select MATCH to match zone 2 settings to zone 1. Press the START/STOP button to begin cooking.
3. Meanwhile, mix the oats, melted butter, brown sugar, and cinnamon to form the topping.
4. Add the topping to the apple halves when they've cooked for 10 minutes.
5. Select zone 1, select BAKE, set temperature to 390°F, and set time to 22 minutes. Select MATCH to match zone 2 settings to zone 1. Press the START/STOP button to begin cooking.
6. Serve warm and enjoy!

Speedy Chocolate Espresso Mini Cheesecake

Servings: 2
Cooking Time: 15 Minutes
Ingredients:

- ½ cup walnuts
- 2 tablespoons salted butter
- 2 tablespoons granular erythritol
- 4 ounces full-fat cream cheese, softened
- 1 large egg
- ½ teaspoon vanilla extract
- 2 tablespoons powdered erythritol
- 2 teaspoons unsweetened cocoa powder
- 1 teaspoon espresso powder

Directions:

1. Put butter, granular erythritol and walnuts in a food processor. Pulse until all the ingredients stick together to form a dough.
2. Place dough into 4&quot| springform pan and put into the air fryer basket.
3. Set the temperature to 400°F, then set the timer for 5 minutes.
4. When timer goes off, remove crust and allow it to cool.
5. Combine cream cheese with vanilla extract, egg, powdered erythritol, espresso powder and cocoa powder until smooth in a medium bowl.
6. Pour mixture on top of baked walnut crust and put into the air fryer basket.
7. Set the temperature for 300°F, then set the timer for 10 minutes.
8. Once fully cooked, allow to chill for 2 hours before serving.

Lemon Sugar Cookie Bars

Monster Sugar Cookie Bars

Servings:12
Cooking Time: 18 Minutes
Ingredients:

- FOR THE LEMON COOKIE BARS
- Grated zest and juice of 1 lemon
- ½ cup granulated sugar
- 4 tablespoons (½ stick) unsalted butter, at room temperature
- 1 large egg yolk
- 1 teaspoon vanilla extract
- ⅛ teaspoon baking powder
- ½ cup plus 2 tablespoons all-purpose flour
- FOR THE MONSTER COOKIE BARS
- ½ cup granulated sugar
- 4 tablespoons (½ stick) unsalted butter, at room temperature
- 1 large egg yolk
- 1 teaspoon vanilla extract
- ⅛ teaspoon baking powder
- ½ cup plus 2 tablespoons all-purpose flour
- ¼ cup rolled oats
- ¼ cup M&M's
- ¼ cup peanut butter chips

Directions:

1. To prep the lemon cookie bars: In a large bowl, rub together the lemon zest and sugar. Add the butter and use a hand mixer to beat until light and fluffy.
2. Beat in the egg yolk, vanilla, and lemon juice. Mix in the baking powder and flour.
3. To prep the monster cookie bars: In a large bowl, with a hand mixer, beat the sugar and butter until light and fluffy.
4. Beat in the egg yolk and vanilla. Mix in the baking powder and flour. Stir in the oats, M&M's, and peanut butter chips.
5. To cook the cookie bars: Line both baskets with aluminum foil. Press the lemon cookie dough into the Zone 1 basket and insert the basket in the unit. Press the monster cookie dough into the Zone 2 basket and insert the basket in the unit.
6. Select Zone 1, select BAKE, set the temperature to 330°F, and set the timer to 18 minutes. Press MATCH COOK to match Zone 2 settings to Zone 1.
7. Press START/PAUSE to begin cooking.
8. When cooking is complete, the cookies should be set in the middle and have begun to pull away from the sides of the basket.
9. Let the cookies cool completely, about 1 hour. Cut each basket into 6 bars for a total of 12 bars.

Nutrition:

- (Per serving) Calories: 191; Total fat: 8.5g; Saturated fat: 5g; Carbohydrates: 27g; Fiber: 0.5g; Protein: 2g; Sodium: 3mg

Pumpkin Muffins

Servings:4
Cooking Time:20

Ingredients:

- 1 and ½ cups of all-purpose flour
- ½ teaspoon baking soda
- ½ teaspoon of baking powder
- 1 and 1/4 teaspoons cinnamon, groaned
- 1/4 teaspoon ground nutmeg, grated
- 2 large eggs
- Salt, pinch
- 3/4 cup granulated sugar
- 1/2 cup dark brown sugar
- 1 and 1/2 cups of pumpkin puree
- 1/4 cup coconut milk

Directions:

1. Take 4 ramekins that are the size of a cup and layer them with muffin papers.
2. Crack an egg in a bowl and add brown sugar, baking soda, baking powder, cinnamon, nutmeg, and sugar.
3. Whisk it all very well with an electric hand beater.
4. Now, in a second bowl, mix the flour, and salt.
5. Now, mix the dry ingredients slowly with the wet ingredients.
6. Now, at the end fold in the pumpkin puree and milk, mix it well
7. Divide this batter into 4 ramekins.
8. Now, divide ramekins between both zones.
9. Set the time for zone 1 to 18 minutes at 360 degrees Fat AIRFRY mode.
10. Select the MATCH button for the zone 2 basket.
11. Check if not done, and let it AIR FRY for one more minute.
12. Once it is done, serve.

Nutrition:

- (Per serving) Calories 291| Fat6.4 g| Sodium 241mg | Carbs 57.1g | Fiber 4.4g | Sugar42 g | Protein 5.9g

Biscuit Doughnuts

Servings: 8
Cooking Time: 15 Minutes

Ingredients:

- ½ cup white sugar
- 1 teaspoon cinnamon
- ½ cup powdered sugar
- 1 can pre-made biscuit dough
- Coconut oil
- Melted butter to brush biscuits

Directions:

1. Place all the biscuits on a cutting board and cut holes in the center of each biscuit using a cookie cutter.
2. Grease the crisper plate with coconut oil.
3. Place the biscuits in the two crisper plates while keeping them 1 inch apart.
4. Return the crisper plates to the Tefal Dual Zone Air Fryer.
5. Choose the Air Fry mode for Zone 1 and set the temperature to 375 degrees F and the time to 15 minutes.
6. Select the "MATCH" button to copy the settings for Zone 2.
7. Initiate cooking by pressing the START/STOP button.
8. Brush all the donuts with melted butter and sprinkle cinnamon and sugar on top.
9. Air fry these donuts for one minute more.
10. Enjoy!

Bread Pudding

Servings: 2
Cooking Time: 15 Minutes

Ingredients:

- Nonstick spray, for greasing ramekins
- 2 slices of white bread, crumbled
- 4 tablespoons white sugar
- 5 large eggs
- ½ cup cream
- Salt, pinch
- ⅓ teaspoon cinnamon powder

Directions:

1. Take a bowl and whisk eggs in it.
2. Add sugar and salt to the eggs and whisk it all well.
3. Then add cream and use a hand beater to incorporate the Ingredients:.
4. Next add cinnamon, and the crumbled white bread.
5. Mix it well and add into two round shaped baking pans.
6. Place each baking pan in the air fryer basket.
7. Set zone 1 to AIR FRY mode at 350 degrees F for 8-12 minutes.
8. Press MATCH button for zone 2.
9. Once it's cooked, serve.

Banana Spring Rolls With Hot Fudge Dip

Servings:4

Cooking Time: 10 Minutes

Ingredients:

- FOR THE BANANA SPRING ROLLS
- 1 large banana
- 4 egg roll wrappers
- 4 teaspoons light brown sugar
- Nonstick cooking spray
- FOR THE HOT FUDGE DIP
- ¼ cup sweetened condensed milk
- 2 tablespoons semisweet chocolate chips
- 1 tablespoon unsweetened cocoa powder
- 1 tablespoon unsalted butter
- ⅛ teaspoon kosher salt
- ⅛ teaspoon vanilla extract

Directions:

1. To prep the banana spring rolls: Peel the banana and halve it crosswise. Cut each piece in half lengthwise, for a total of 4 pieces.
2. Place one piece of banana diagonally across an egg roll wrapper. Sprinkle with 1 teaspoon of brown sugar. Fold the edges of the egg roll wrapper over the ends of the banana, then roll to enclose the banana inside. Brush the edge of the wrapper with water and press to seal. Spritz with cooking spray. Repeat with the remaining bananas, egg roll wrappers, and brown sugar.
3. To prep the hot fudge dip: In an ovenproof ramekin or bowl, combine the condensed milk, chocolate chips, cocoa powder, butter, salt, and vanilla.
4. To cook the spring rolls and hot fudge dip: Install a crisper plate in each of the two baskets. Place the banana spring rolls seam-side down in the Zone 1 basket and insert the basket in the unit. Place the ramekin in the Zone 2 basket and insert the basket in the unit.
5. Select Zone 1, select AIR FRY, set the temperature to 390°F, and set the timer to 10 minutes.
6. Select Zone 2, select BAKE, set the temperature to 330°F, and set the timer to 8 minutes. Select SMART FINISH.
7. Press START/PAUSE to begin cooking.
8. When the Zone 2 timer reads 3 minutes, press START/PAUSE. Remove the basket and stir the hot fudge until smooth. Reinsert the basket and press START/PAUSE to resume cooking.
9. When cooking is complete, the spring rolls should be crisp.
10. Let the hot fudge cool for 2 to 3 minutes. Serve the banana spring rolls with hot fudge for dipping.

Nutrition:

- (Per serving) Calories: 268; Total fat: 10g; Saturated fat: 4g; Carbohydrates: 42g; Fiber: 2g; Protein: 5g; Sodium: 245mg

Monkey Bread

Servings: 12

Cooking Time: 10 Minutes

Ingredients:

- Bread
- 12 Rhodes white dinner rolls
- ½ cup brown sugar
- 1 teaspoon cinnamon
- 4 tablespoons butter melted
- Glaze
- ½ cup powdered sugar
- 1-2 tablespoons milk
- ½ teaspoon vanilla

Directions:

1. Mix brown sugar, cinnamon and butter in a bowl.
2. Cut the dinner rolls in half and dip them in the sugar mixture.
3. Place these buns in a greased baking pan and pour the remaining butter on top.
4. Place the buns in the air fryer baskets.
5. Return the air fryer basket 1 to Zone 1, and basket 2 to Zone 2 of the Tefal 2-Basket Air Fryer.
6. Choose the "Air Fry" mode for Zone 1 at 350 degrees F and 10 minutes of cooking time.
7. Initiate cooking by pressing the START/PAUSE BUTTON.
8. Flip the rolls once cooked halfway through.
9. Meanwhile, mix milk, vanilla and sugar in a bowl.
10. Pour the glaze over the air fried rolls.
11. Serve.

Nutrition:

- (Per serving) Calories 192 | Fat 9.3g |Sodium 133mg | Carbs 27.1g | Fiber 1.4g | Sugar 19g | Protein 3.2g

Air Fryer Sweet Twists

Servings: 2
Cooking Time: 10 Minutes

Ingredients:

- 1 box store-bought puff pastry
- ½ teaspoon cinnamon
- ½ teaspoon sugar
- ½ teaspoon black sesame seeds
- Salt, pinch
- 2 tablespoons Parmesan cheese, freshly grated

Directions:

1. Place the dough on a work surface.
2. Take a small bowl and mix in cheese, sugar, salt, sesame seeds, and cinnamon.
3. Press this mixture on both sides of the dough.
4. Now, cut the pastry into 1" x 3" strips.
5. Twist each of the strips twice from each end.
6. Transfer them to both the air fryer baskets.
7. Select zone 1 to AIR FRY mode at 400 degrees F for 9-10 minutes.
8. Select the MATCH button for the zone 2 basket.
9. Once cooked, serve.

Honey Lime Pineapple

Servings: 4
Cooking Time: 10 Minutes

Ingredients:

- 562g pineapple chunks
- 55g brown sugar
- 30ml lime juice
- 63g honey

Directions:

1. In a bowl, mix pineapple, honey, lime juice, and brown sugar. Cover and place in refrigerator for 1 hour.
2. Insert a crisper plate in Tefal air fryer baskets.
3. Remove pineapple chunks from the marinade and place in both baskets.
4. Select zone 1 then select "air fry" mode and set the temperature to 390 degrees F for 10 minutes. Press "match" to match zone 2 settings to zone 1. Press "start/stop" to begin. Stir halfway through.

Nutrition:

- (Per serving) Calories 153 | Fat 0.2g |Sodium 5mg | Carbs 40.5g | Fiber 2g | Sugar 35.7g | Protein 0.8g

Chocó Lava Cake

Servings: 4
Cooking Time: 10 Minutes

Ingredients:

- 3 eggs
- 3 egg yolks
- 70g dark chocolate, chopped
- 168g cups powdered sugar
- 96g all-purpose flour
- 1 tsp vanilla
- 113g butter
- ½ tsp salt

Directions:

1. Add chocolate and butter to a bowl and microwave for 30 seconds. Remove from oven and stir until smooth.
2. Add eggs, egg yolks, sugar, flour, vanilla, and salt into the melted chocolate and stir until well combined.
3. Pour batter into the four greased ramekins.
4. Insert a crisper plate in Tefal air fryer baskets.
5. Place ramekins in both baskets.
6. Select zone 1 then select "air fry" mode and set the temperature to 390 degrees F for 10 minutes. Press "match" to match zone 2 settings to zone 1. Press "start/stop" to begin.

Nutrition:

- (Per serving) Calories 687 | Fat 37.3g |Sodium 527mg | Carbs 78.3g | Fiber 1.5g | Sugar 57.4g | Protein 10.7g

Fruity Blackberry Crisp

Servings: 4
Cooking Time: 15 Minutes
Ingredients:

- 2 cups blackberries
- ⅓ cup powdered erythritol
- 2 tablespoons lemon juice
- ¼ teaspoon xanthan gum
- 1 cup Crunchy Granola

Directions:

1. Mix erythritol, blackberries, xanthan gum, and lemon juice in a large bowl.
2. Place into 6&quot| round baking dish and cover with a sheet of foil. Put into the air fryer basket.
3. Set the temperature to 350°F, then set the timer for 12 minutes.
4. When the goes off, remove the foil and shake well.
5. Sprinkle granola on the top of mixture and place back to the air fryer basket.
6. Set the temperature to 320°F, then set the timer for 3 minutes or until the top is golden brown.
7. Serve immediately.

Simple Cheesecake

Servings: 3
Cooking Time: 20 Minutes
Ingredients:

- ½ egg
- 2 tablespoons sugar
- ⅛ teaspoon vanilla extract
- ¼ cup honey graham cracker crumbs
- ½ tablespoon unsalted butter, softened
- ¼ pound cream cheese, softened

Directions:

1. Line a round baking dish with parchment paper.
2. For crust: In a bowl, add the graham cracker crumbs and butter.
3. Place the crust into baking dish and press to smooth.
4. Press "Zone 1" and "Zone 2" and then rotate the knob for each zone to select "Bake".
5. Set the temperature to 350 degrees F/ 175 degrees C for both zones and then set the time for 5 minutes to preheat.
6. After preheating, arrange the baking dish into the basket of each zone.
7. Slide each basket into Air Fryer and set the time for 4 minutes.
8. Remove the crust from the oven and set aside to cool slightly.
9. Meanwhile, take a bowl, add the cream cheese and sugar. Whisk until smooth.
10. Now, place the eggs, one at a time and whisk until mixture becomes creamy.
11. Add the vanilla extract and mix well.
12. Place the cream cheese mixture evenly over the crust.
13. Arrange the baking dish into the Air-Fryer basket.
14. Remove from the oven and set aside to cool.
15. Serve and enjoy!

RECIPES INDEX

C

I

J

K

L

M

N

O

P

Q

R

S

T

V

W

Z

Printed in Great Britain
by Amazon

40740198R00059